FAMILY LIFE EDUCATION FOR ADOLESCENT GIRLS

FAMILY LIFE EDUCATION FOR ADOLESCENT GIRLS

D. SARADA

1999
Discovery Publishing House
New Delhi-110 002

First Published – 1999

Reprinted – 2026

ISBN: 978-81-7141-499-4

Family Life Education for Adolescent Girls

Published by:

DISCOVERY PUBLISHING HOUSE
4383/4B, Ansari Road, Darya Ganj
New Delhi-110 002 (India)
Phone: +91-11-23279245; 23253475; 43596065
Mobile: +91 9811179893 / +91 9871656464
E-mail: discoverybooksindia@gmail.com
orderdphbooks@gmail.com
namitwasan9@gmail.com
web: www.discoverypublishinggroup.com

Printed at:
Infinity Imaging Systems
Delhi

Foreword

Family Life Education is fast growing as a subject in several directions over the last few decades. People around the world have come to realise the significance of family once again. Family as an institution needs to be perserved to serve as a centre for human growth and development. The individuals and their capabilities are the very thing on which nations are built, such individuals are born and brought up in Families. The families of today are exposed to various forces of change both internal and external, which brought changes in the family structure and continues to pose a threat to the family system.

Rapid technological developments, increased mobility, new employment and work structure, academic and career aspirations of parents is leading to alienation of children from their homes, parents and the elderly. The children are increasingly becoming ignorant of familial tasks and are unable to behave 'correctly' as family members. This failure may lead to deprivations and affects the family equilibrium. Realising this danger, education in family occupations was conceptualised as a solution, which is called Family Life Education.

Family Life Education is introduced widely as an intervention programme by drawing information from various related disciplines. Yet its content and methodologies seem to vary depending on the requirements of the group. There are not many systematic researches conducted in this areas and very few books are published on this subject. The author has aptly chosen this area, which is attracting considerable attention for indepth study in the realm of Family studies after she made several successful endeavours to devise steps to make this subject of FLE as a field of specialisation for Ph.D., and other research and extension programmes. This will be of benefit to teachers and students, community educators working in the area of Family Life Education.

In this book the author has covered conceptual issues and experimental studies on family concepts, structure, transition, problems, changes and future, women: role in the family, work structure, problems and changes, adolescents: developmental tasks, problems and future, family life education; need, programmes and content, educational system; analysis of channels of education for reaching unreached adolescents. The highlight of the book is the methodologies developed to formulate curriculum in the form of a manual. Development of relevant tools for measurement of variables under study is a scientific technique and this has received careful attention of the author. As the book is based on a participatory action research, all the aspects have been appropriately discussed and presented in this book. It will be helpful as a reference book and also as a practical resource guide for all those involved in teaching/training/communicating family life education.

Prof. A. Sathyavathi,
Formerly Principal,
Sri Padmavathi Mahila
Viswavidyalayam,
Tirupati- 517 502. A.P.

Acknowledgement

In the preparation of this book, I have received help, advice and guidance from several quarters. At the outset, I wish to express my deep sense of gratitude to my former guide Late Dr. (Ms) Anna Mathew, but for whose whole-hearted support and co-operation, the book would not have come out in the present form.

I am extremely grateful to my present research supervisor Dr. (Ms.) K. Chandralekha, Professor and Head, Department of Home Science, whose expert guidance and valuable suggestions have been responsible for the completion of the study.

I am also thankful to Dr. V.L.N. Reddy, formerly Professor and Head, Dept. of Adult Education, S.V. University; Dr. Venkatarami Reddy, formerly Professor and Head, Dept. of Education, S.V. University and Dr. S. Padmanabhaiah, Reader, Dept. of Education, S.V. University for their advice and valuable suggestions.

I am indebted to the heads of the following institutions for the valuable information and materials rendered for the research work : National Institute of Adult Education, New Delhi; National Institute for Educational Planning and Administration, New Delhi; State Resource Centre, Hyderabad; Family Planning Association of India, Bombay; Department of Education, Chittoor District (A.P.); District Institute for Educational Training, Karveti Nagaram, Chittoor District (A.P.).

I am also grateful to the librarians of : Sri Padmavati Mahila Visvavidyalayam Library, Tirupati; Madras Institute of Social Work Library, Madras; Tata Institute of Social Science Library, Bombay; National Institute of Public Co-operation and Child Development Library, New Delhi; National Institute for Rural Development Library, Hyderabad and S.V. University Library, Tirupati.

I would be failing in my duty, if I do not acknowledge my gratitude to Dr. P. Kusuma Kumari, Professor and Head, Department of Telugu Studies for the expertise rendered in Telugu translation.

My sincere thanks are due to all the experts and the respondents who have participated in the study, without whose co-operation the study could not have completed.

My thanks are also due to Dr. A. Sathyavathi, Principal, University College, Sri Padmavati Mahila Visvavidyalayam, Tirupati for her co-operation.

I acknowledge with thanks the help of Mr. Raghavendra, Irace Computers and Mr. Karthik, Siddhartha Photostats, Tirupati, for their promptness and expertise in computation. I extend my thanks to Mr. Lakshmana Rao, Artist for preparing the illustrations for the FLE manual.

My indebtedness is beyond words to my husband, Sri K. Raghunatha Reddy, for his encouragement, patience and continuous help and to my children who were denied the care and comforts due to my preoccupation with research.

I am also grateful to my parents and friends for their co-operation and encouragement throughout the study.

D. SARADA

Contents

Foreword v
Acknowledgement vii
List of Abbreviations xi
1. Introduction 1
   Statement of the Problem
   Objectives of the Study
   Hypotheses
2. Review of Relevant Literature 9
   Conceptual Issues on Family Significance
   Conceptual Issues on Family Transition of Indian Family
   Conceptual Issues on Women and Family
   Conceptual Issues on Adolescent and Family Life Education
   Achieving Emotional Independence of Parents
   Conceptual Issues on Non-formal Adult Education Programme (NFAEP)
   Family Life Education in India : A Historical Review
   Family Life Education : Concept and Need
   Major Observations
3. Methodology 50
   Research Design
   Locale of the Study
   Sample Selection
   Variables Selection
   Relationship Among the Independent and Dependent Variables

Assessment of Variables
Tools of the Study
Statistical Analysis of Data
Operational Definition of the Concept Used in the Study Family Life Education (FLE)
4. Results and Discussion 66
Demographic Profile of Respondents
Respondents Exposure to FLE Information
Identification of FLE Needs
Impact of Socio-economic Background of Married Women and Unmarried Adolescent Girls on FLE Need Perceptions
Family Income and FLE Need Perception
Marital Status and FLE Need Perception
Content Analysis of NAEP Primers of Chittoor District (Andhra Pradesh)
FLE Manual
Impact of FLE Programme on NAEP Participants
5. Summary and Conclusion 113
Introduction
Statement of the Problem
Objective of the Study
Hypotheses
Research Design
Locale of the Study
Sample Selection
Variables
Tools of the Study
Assessment of Variables
Statistical Analysis of Data
Salient Findings
Conclusion
Bibliography 125
Appendix 134
Index 183

List of Abbreviations

FLE	:	Family Life Education
FLEP	:	Family Life Education Programme
NFAEP	:	Non-formal Adult Education Programme
NAEP	:	National Adult Education Programme
AEP	:	Adult Education Programme
IPCL	:	Improved Pace and Content of Learning
SRC	:	State Resource Centre
FPAI	:	Family Planning Association of India
MPFL	:	Mass Programme for Functional Literacy
JSN	:	Janasikshana Nilayams
DIET	:	District Institute for Education and Training

1

Introduction

"The hand that rocks the cradle, rules the world" is a maxim well known to everyone, but a few realise the full implications of it. The years before a woman becomes a mother are the crucial years, when she prepares herself for this important role of motherhood. Her abilities—physical, emotional and intellectual—determine the quality of life she holds for her children. Hence, it is important that efforts should be made to see that girls particularly in their adolescence are given the necessary education to play their role effectively as mothers, that is the education for family life.

The adolescence is the period of physical, psychological and social maturing from childhood to adulthood. According to the joint statements issued by the WHO/UNFPA/UNICEF in 1989, the development that takes place in adolescence is generally uneven. These young girls are the most crucial segment of global populations from the point of view of the 'quality' of future generation who are on the threshold of marriage and motherhood. The statements further added that FLE assumes importance in view of the fact that majority of the rural girls are illiterate.

According to various studies conducted in 1989, population of adolescents (10-19 years) in India was 22.5 per cent of the total population. The distribution of rural and urban population of adolescents was 78.4 and 21.6 per cent, respectively. Eminent scientists have urged for a high priority to be given to the adolescent girls in order to overcome the problem of low birth weight and improve maternal nutritional status as well as to reduce maternal morbidity rate. Gopalan (1990) has made concrete suggestions towards focusing attention on these young girls. He has advocated "Education for better living and vocational training for rural adolescent girls".

Rao (1988) considered the adolescence stage as a traumatic period. Educational centres, state bodies, social welfare and family welfare centres, and other agencies in the west planned certain programmes and courses which resulted in the development of the specialist fields of sex education and family life education. In India, through a few social and family welfare agencies, particularly the Family Planning Association of India, a voluntary body dedicated to the promotion of family planning, has been conducting family life education programmes. But the subject however, has not gained the prominence it deserves.

According to Wadia (1980), the term 'Family Life Education' (FLE) still awaits a precise definition, especially in the Indian context. FLE imparts not only factual knowledge, where the reproductive system and processes are explained in a simple scientific way (and about which ignorance is widespread even among those who are married and are parents) but it also involves value systems, or rather, it involves developing a capacity to work out values, and to have the conviction and strength to abide by them. There are, of course, many other emotional, psychological and relational factors which can help in the attainment of personal satisfaction and fulfilment. The term FLE, therefore, is a more comprehensive one, for, it can include not only sex education but a wide gamut of family and interpersonal relationships which are so important especially in the Indian society. Wadia (1980) has further stated that young people need knowledge and education not only about the physical manifestations of the population problem but also about human sexuality and their reactions, if they are to respond in a constructive way to the challenges facing them in their adult world of tomorrow. Family life education (FLE), which relates to a wide range of issues in the daily lives at the familial level, has emerged as a discipline drawing information from various disciplines such as population education, home science, social work, adult education and women's studies.

Family life education, with its objective of increasing satisfaction from family living, is receiving increasingly greater attention all over the world. In the advanced, affluent countries, the institution of family faces numerous tensions and threats arising out of complexities of modern living. In these countries, family life education has a distinct socio-psychological connotation and is provided mainly through family counselling and specialized courses. On the other hand, in a developing country like India, where conditions of poverty and ignorance are rampant, and where the pressures and strains of life relate to mobilizing the basic resources necessary for existence, this concept assumes different ramifications (Kapoor, 1986). Family Planning Association of India (FPAI) has pioneered the introduction of FLE in India.

The Family Planning Association of India (FPAI), a national voluntary organisation is devoted to promoting knowledge of family planning as a basic 'human right' as well as population policies, which can bring about a balanced development of the resources of the country—both human and material—as a means towards raising the quality of life (Wadia, 1969).

In the year 1951, the Government of India sponsored a National Family Planning Programme to control population growth. The programme which was later merged with maternal and child health services as family planning programme, centred around the mother and the child. Further, this integrated approach was also strengthened by the 'All India Post Partum Programme' in the year 1967 to promote contraceptive acceptance among women coming to Government hospitals for delivery or abortion.

National Family Planning programme received a serious set back due to the excesses committed in mass sterilisation camps in 1970. In order to tone down the reaction to the excesses in the family planning programme, it was renamed as 'Family Welfare Programme', wherein family planning has been perceived as an integral part of comprehensive policy covering education, health, maternity and child care, family welfare, women's rights and nutrition. Massive educational and motivational drives have been launched to promote the programme (Ministry of Health and Family Welfare, 1978).

Over the years, the FPAI extended population education programmes to schools, colleges and universities, while at the same time carrying out special programmes geared to the larger and much neglected out of school sector. The programmes have grown in scope, quality and coverage and, in keeping with educational needs, have widened to include family life and sex education in suitable cases since Fifth Five Year Plan (1974-78).

The population issue which so closely influences quality of human life and which ultimately is controlled by personal family decision-making, within the close family, is the important reason for integrating family life related issues with population education. Population education and family life education are educationally conceptualised to have natural and logical linkages with each other. They represent two dimensions of viewing people's lives within a cup of everyday life issues in the context of the contemporary world. The focus in population education is the aggregate at macro level which relates to the statistical formulations of the broader population environment dynamics operating within the total developmental perspective (Merh, 1984).

In the scheme of these interactions, at the micro level, the individual and the family occupy an important logical and structural position. The features that are reflected in the population are the results of actions and events that take place at the family level. Population characteristics such as size, distribution, age structure, sex ratio, events such as marriage, birth, death, migration, qualitative components in terms of health, wealth, education, food, employment, social welfare, social justice, human dignity, human rights and inter-personal relations, all have their reflections at the micro level. For instance, large population is a reflection of larger families in the context of the level of socio-cultural and economic development of a given society. The concept of 'Family' in population, links the demographic with the socio-cultural and psychological aspects of human matters. Thus, it relates to persons. The efforts in both postulates is towards the improvement of human conditions and integration and enrichment of human life inclusive of the improvement and preservation of the total environment (Merh, 1984).

The expressions 'Population Education' (PE) and 'Family Life Education' (FLE) till date have been used interchangeably and flexibly in developing a variety of programmes in different countries of the world. A synoptic review of population education literature since its inception in 1969 to date bears out this fact (Merh, 1984). In programmes that are being formulated in recent years, wherever the point of reference, is family education. An effort is made to encompass the ecological, social and developmental aspects as they relate to family matters. Even though conceptual clarity with regard to FLE is gradually emerging, due to inadequate information and data base, absence of scientific and quantitative indicators, lack of integration of knowledge base pertaining to the specifics of the Indian situation have slowed its progress.

FLE is perceived to be usually operating through informal channels of education which incidentally everyone receives. FLE seems to be a learning process that begins almost at birth and continues throughout life. FLE is not to be confused with sex education, for it is much broader in scope, though sex education, is part of it. The complexity of today's cultural milieu, the multiplicity of forces working upon the individual, the widening inter generational gaps require an educational approach which is likely to help different members of the family to assess his or her role to create a harmony and strength in the family unit (Merh, 1984).

The programmes conducted by FPAI are restricted by the time allotted to them by schools, which naturally results in a concentration on imparting only a certain amount of knowledge or only certain dimensions of knowledge. To obtain sound results, a scientifically planned curriculum of FLE based on the adolescent's needs and requirements should be introduced in schools either as a separate subject or as a part of the school curriculum (Rao, 1988).

Many programmes have been conceived and implemented in India for extension education of women. Notably, FLE is an important constituent of most of such programmes. Their objectives have been defined and accordingly, their contents have been conceptualized. In actual implementation, no programme provides FLE except Grihini Training Programmes. Grihini training programmes are intended for tribal girls in Bihar, Madhya Pradesh, West Bengal, Orissa and Maharashtra (Kapoor, 1986). In these programmes, issues related to family planning, small family norm, health and nutrition were included.

The factors responsible for the FLE activities not having been conducted in the spirit and to the extent they ought to have, were revealed in a study conducted by Kapoor (1986). The factors are three fold; first, the factors that relate to the physical facilities available in the centres; second, those that pertain to the field level functionaries; and third, those that concern the supervision and guidance given to field level functionaries. This indicates that there is a great need to reinforce and strengthen the existing extension education programmes in order to impart FLE to the needy groups.

Population and family life related issues were not considered to be within the purview of home science until recently. A survey of home science colleges and their involvement in family planning and population education related activities conducted by Verma indicates that it has been a common practice to involve a doctor or public health person to give lectures on specific topics, i.e., contraception or family planning methods, etc., included in courses such as Marriage and Family relations, Adolescent Development, which are taught in home science colleges (Verma, 1980). In 1971, the American Home Economics Association (AHEA) brought together a group of international home economists to discuss the need for home economists around the world, to actively involve themselves in programmes dealing with family planning, population education and quality of life of individuals and families. In 1974, the international family planning project of the American Home Economics Association and the International Planned Parenthood Federation (IPPF) was launched and a series of workshops, seminars and summer institutes were organised with the objective of bringing about greater involvement of home economics in this field. The field of Home science focuses on the family, its dynamics and the interrelationship within it. It aims at promoting the quality of life of individuals and families in communities.

Though some sporadic efforts have been made in India by various organisations and academic institutions to impart family life education to needy groups, there were not many programmes planned and organised on the basis of scientific research. Planning and implementation of FLE programmes for India's younger generation calls for assessment of existing educational infrastructure. Education usually involves contact with teachers for many hours, each day, over many years of one's life. The educational system, with inadequate school facilities and a programme irrelevant to a vast majority, keeps out almost 2 per cent of the nation's children. While 20 per cent do not go to school at all, 50 per cent of those who go to school quit in the first standard itself, 60 per cent abandon it before the fifth standard (age 11), and 75 per cent before the eighth standard (age 14). The drop out rate is extremely high. Since three to four years of schooling are required for lasting literacy, the majority who drop out of school relapse into illiteracy (Saraswathi, 1984; Mali, 1984; Ramabramham, 1988; Singh, 1989; Sivadasan, 1990).

From the foregoing facts, it is evident that the system of formal education caters only to a small percentage of the population. The existing system is perpetuated by promoting the values of competition, inequality and individual self-interest essentially by focusing on subject matter learning and by measuring success through examination results, with little or no respect given to the learner, his needs, interests and capabilities. In this context, non-formal education has emerged as an alternative in recent times stressing the values of co-operation, equality and group solidarity (Saraswathi, 1984).

With the emergence of a powerful alternative non-formal educational system, this problem of spending several years at school is solved. Non-formal adult education is essentially a process of learning through reflection and through sharing of experience by participants. The NAEP has identified illiterates in the age group of 15-35 years as the target group. This coincides in substantial and convenient measure with the target groups for FLE although FLE can start at a much younger age. The decision, therefore, to incorporate FLE in the NAEP, if implemented with drive and thoroughness, can mean a tremendous boost to both the programmes. The present study aims at utilising the non-formal adult education programme for imparting family life education. FLE programme can assist the unreached young generation in strengthening their family lives. FLE is intended for adolescent girls as education for better living.

The focus of the study, as pointed out earlier, is an assessment of the needs of family life education and development of FLE curriculum for adolescent girls through the non-formal adult education programme in Chittoor district of Andhra Pradesh.

Statement of the Problem

Family Life Education for Adolescent Girls Through the Non-Formal Adult Education Programme

Objectives of the Study

- Identification of the FLE needs of adolescent learners of NFAEP as perceived by the learners themselves; married adult women and the subject experts.
- Assessment of the factors causing differential FLE need perceptions of married adult women, experts and unmarried adolescent girls.
- To assess the impact of age, family income, caste, type of family, size of the family and marital status on FLE need perception of the unmarried adolescent learners of NFAEP.
- Examination of the adequacy and relevance of FLE content in the NFAEP.
- Development of a model FLE curriculum for unmarried adolescent girls and
- Evaluation of effectiveness of model FLE curriculum for adolescent girls.

Hypotheses

In order to accomplish the foregoing objectives, the following hypotheses were formulated and tested.

1. The FLE need perceptions of adolescent girls, married adult women and subject experts are significantly different from each other.
2. The FLE need perception of adolescent girls and married adult women is significantly influenced by their socio-economic background.
3. The coverage of FLE information in NFAEP primers is not adequate.
4. A need based curriculum has a significant impact on the FLE status of unmarried adolescent girls.

2

Review of Relevant Literature

The literature on FLE in India is scanty. Not many comprehensive studies have been conducted on different dimensions of FLE. However, elements of FLE are found in several studies on Indian family, adult education programmes, population studies and gender studies. An attempt was made in this chapter to review these studies with a view to assess their contribution and identify the gaps in the literature.

Conceptual Issues on Family Significance

The intense emotional meaning of family for almost everyone has been observed throughout history. Philosophers and social analysts have noted that any society is a structure made up of families linked together. The earliest moral and ethical writings of many cultures assert the significance of the family within those commentaries, the view is often expressed that a society loses its strength if people do not fulfil family obligations. Confucius thought that happiness and prosperity would prevail if everyone would behave "correctly" as a family member. This meant primarily that no one should fail in his familial obligations. That is, the proper relationship between a ruler and subjects was one of father and his children. The cultural importance of the family is also emphasized in the Old Testament. The books of Exodus, Deuteronomy, Ecclesiastes, Psalms, and Proverbs, for example, proclaim the importance of obeying family rules. The earliest codified literature in India, the Rig-Veda, which dates back to the last half of the second millennium B.C., and the law of Manu, which dates from about the beginning of the Christian era, devote much attention to the family. Poetry, plays, novels, and short stories, typically seize upon family relationships as the primary focus of human passion, and their ideas and themes often grow from family conflict. Even the great epic poems of war have sub-themes focusing on problems in family relations (Goode, 1987).

The family is only a small part of the social structure of modern industrial societies. It is within the family that the child is first socialised to serve the needs of the society, and not only its own needs. A society will not survive unless its needs are met, such as the production and distribution of commodities, protection of the young and old or the sick and the pregnant, conformity to the law, and so on. Only if individuals are motivated to serve these needs the society will continue to operate and the foundation for that motivation is laid by the family.

The family is made up of individuals, but it is also a social unit, and part of a large social network. Families are not isolated, self-enclosed social systems and the other institutions of society, such as the military, the Church, or the school system, continually rediscover that they are not dealing with individuals, but with members of families. Even in the most industrialised and urban societies, where it is sometimes supposed that people lead rootless and anonymous lives, most people are in continual interaction with other family members (Goode, 1987).

The family is by far the most important institution in a society. Family is the basic unit in which individuals receive most of their personal satisfaction, and in which the personality of the child is formed. It is within the family that the spouses get regular sex satisfaction, children are given nurture and education, food and clothing and the dwelling place of its members is provided. In illness or pregnancy, during child birth, the family renders care. It is the centre of warmth and affection among its members as long as normal health conditions prevail (Friedlander, 1976).

The family is the foundation of the large social structure, in that, all other institutions depend on its contributions (Goode, 1964). The importance of family lies in its functions stated below :

- for most individuals, family serves as the basic socializing agent for the acquisition or internalization of beliefs and attitudes;
- it constitutes the chief source of realisation of personal satisfaction; and
- it serves as a basic instrument of social control (Eshleman, 1974).

According to Kulkarni (1977), family is a link between continuity and change. Besides the individual and the community, it is the family which provides a third dimension of depth to the evolution of human kind. The family determines the development of individuals. Family is also an important source of stability and support when there are problems from the environment. Human development can, therefore, be best enhanced by enriching the family life. This stands in sharp contrast to the picture of the family presented as a source of love, sympathy and support. The family is the only social institution other than religion that is formally developed in all societies. It is a specific social agency incharge of a great variety of social behaviours and activities.

The family is conceived as "A unit of interacting personalities" (Schvaneveldt, 1966). As the family is a system of inter-dependent and reciprocal relationships, the behaviour of any family member affects all others in the family. Family equilibrium and sound interpersonal relationships between family members are important factors for family dynamics (Kashyap, 1993).

Family members also participate in informal social control processes. Socialization at early ages makes most people to conform, but throughout each day, both the children and adults, often deviate. The formal agencies of social control (such as the police) are not enough to do more than force the extreme deviant to conform. What is needed is a set of social pressures that provide feedback to the individual, whenever, he or she, does well or poorly and thus support internal controls as well as the controls of the formal agencies. Effectively or not, the family usually takes on this task (Goode, 1987).

According to the United Nations Report (1987) "Human rights could be generally defined as those rights which are inherent in our nature and without which we cannot live as human beings. Human rights and fundamental freedom allow us to fully develop and use our human qualities, our intelligence, our talents and our spiritual and other needs." The concept of human rights needs to be applied to the family also, for maximization of happiness in family life. Denial of these rights creates conditions of exploitation, deprivation and destitution.

Desai (1993) viewed, human rights with reference to the family at three levels :

- the individual's right to have a family;
- the individual's right within the family; and
- the family's rights with reference to its environment.

The United Nation's instruments on human rights at these three levels were stated as follows :

The Individuals Rights to Have a Family

Every child has the right to be reared by his or her natural family; every parent, has the duty to rear his or her children; and every adult has the right to marry and found a family.

The Individuals Rights Within the Family

Every family member is equal in dignity and rights, irrespective of age, gender and socio-economic status :

(a)
- every family member has an equal allocation of family resources;
- every family member has an equal right to physical care and development through housing, food and health care;
- every family member has an equal right to education and training, free choice of employment, rest and leisure, and opportunities for cultural and moral development;
- every family member has an equal right to participate in community life; and
- every family member has a right to social security in crisis such as Unemployment, disability, illness and in old age.

(b) Every married partner has the right to gender equality in marriage with respect to role, power and status; parenting, guardianship and custody of children, title to matrimonial home and dissolution of marriage.

(c) Every family member has the right to life and security of person
- no family member shall be subjected to arbitrary interference with his or her privacy and to attack upon his or her honour by other family members;
- no family member shall be subjected to torture or to cruel inhuman or degrading treatment or punishment by other family members; and
- no family member shall be held in slavery or servitude by other family members.

(d) Every family member has the right to choices in family life
- every family member has the right to freedom of thought, opinion and expression;

- every adult has the right to choose with reference to the choice of a marriage partner, age at marriage, practices of endogamy and exogamy, marriage rituals, residence, child bearing, adoption and lineage; and
- every family member has a right to choose not to marry and/or not to have children.

(e) Every family member has duties toward the family and may recognize and respect the rights of other family members.

The Family's Rights with Reference to Its Environment

Every family is equal in its dignity and rights, without distinctions of race, colour, language, religion, political or other opinion, national or social origin, property or other status.

(a) every family has right to privacy and freedom of residence and movement. No family shall be held in slavery or servitude;
(b) every family has the right to adequate housing in a healthy environment.
(c) every family and all its members have the right of access to appropriate public services of financial, legal, health, education and training, child care and other systems;
(d) every family member has the right to social security in crisis as disability, chronic terminal illness, ageing of individual members and victimization of the family by political violence and environmental disasters; and
(e) every family and all its members have duties toward its environment, and to protect the rights of other families.

The commentaries of analysts on nature, patterns and types of Indian family are briefly reviewed in the following manner : A family is a group of people who generally live under one roof, who eat cooked in one kitchen, who hold property in common, participate in common family worship and are related to one another as some particular type of kindred (Karve, 1968).

The conceptual issues reviewed above clearly indicate the significance of family. To-day the family no longer performs the tasks effectively once entrusted to it, viz., production, education and projection. The family as a training institution to its members has been undergoing fundamental changes. The studies on changes that have occurred in Indian family system are reviewed in the following section.

Conceptual Issues on Transition of Indian Family

Family may be nuclear or joint. Nuclear family may be defined as the social group, consisting of a married man and woman with their children living together under the same roof and sharing a common hearth. Joint family is defined as the social group, consisting of several related individual families, especially those of a man and his sons (in case of patrilineal system) or of a woman and her daughters (in case of matrimonial system) residing in a single large dwelling or a cluster of small ones.

The fundamental characteristic of traditional Hindu family is its joint nature. Besides being joint in structure, the Hindu family has been patriarchal, patrilineal, patrilocal and monogamous in nature. The possibility of matrilocal joint families cannot be completely ruled out but such cases are quite exceptional. Such families are only common among the Nayars of Kerala. Thus, it can be said that in the Hindu Society the traditionally approved family form has been the patriarchal joint family system (Sahay, 1969).

In contrast to this, Desai (1994) stated that the joint family is known as the prototype of the Indian family system. It is important to understand that joint family as an institution developed for preservation of family property and therefore, prevalent mainly among the upper class and upper caste families. Hindu scriptures that have promoted the joint family norms have been written by upper caste Brahmins. Even sociological literature on family studies have focused mainly on the joint family, ignoring other family forms among other castes and classes, reflected in the anthropological literature.

The prominent focus of family studies in India has also been on whether joint family is breaking down as a result of industrialisation and urbanisation when the joint family system was prevalent only among a minority of the population, and when urbanism existed in India prior to industrialisation, the question whether industrialisation and urbanisation have led to its break up is out of place.

The traditional Indian family which has been characterized as joint family must have emerged as early as the Vedic period in an agrarian society based on plough cultivation. The village was almost an economically self sufficient unit producing sufficient food for its survival. The occupational structure of the village was also quite simple. There was only one occupation for the village and that was agriculture. There were, no doubt, the artisan classes also living in the village such as carpenters, smiths, potters, weavers, etc., but, their occupation was closely allied to agriculture. In fact, it was a corollary of the agricultural occupation. Mobility was hardly necessary for economic survival in the social setting of agrarian economy. This then was an ideal setting for an institution like joint family with its emphasis on common living. But the circumstances under which the institution flourished in the traditional Hindu Society could not ever remain the same. As Kapadia (1972) has pointed out "with the advent of the British, a transformation of cultural pattern became inevitable by virtue of the new forces generated by them—administrative, ideological and economic". The villages are no more self sufficient, as the agrarian base of the Indian society is now in the process of transformation. India's contact with the West during the British rule led to the induction of a number of modern ideas and values into the Hindu society, and the process of transformation which thus began has been further invigorated during the post Independence phase as a result of planning and development. The traditional Hindu joint family has, thus lost its natural base and is faced with the problem of survival (Parmar, 1987).

The normative family patterns in India are extended or joint family and elementary or nuclear family. The term joint family is used more commonly in India than extended family. The joint family comprises of two or more elementary families, bound together by common movable or immovable property, and may or may not be staying together (Desai, 1993). According to Gore (1968), in a developing country such as India, it is more fruitful to view a joint family as a group consisting of adult male coparceners and their dependents, as these families do not necessarily comprise of two or more distinct nuclear family units. Variations in a joint family are lineal joint families, collateral joint families and lineal-cum-collateral joint families (Kolenda, 1987). Gore (1968) termed lineal joint families as filial joint families and collateral joint families as fraternal joint families. A joint household means a joint family living together.

The elementary or nuclear family comprises of couples and their unmarried children, and is generally financially independent of other families (Desai, 1956). A variation of an elementary/ nuclear family is the supplemented nuclear family which comprises of the nuclear family with single relatives (Kolenda, 1987). A nuclear household means a nuclear family living together, which may or may not be financially independent of other families.

Leslie and Korman (1984) termed extended families as consanguineal families as they focus on blood relations. They termed nuclear families as conjugal families as the conjugal relation is the core of these families. Buroes and Locke (1950) used the terms institutional family and companionship family for joint and nuclear families respectively.

As an institution, the family is based on more or less formal rules and regulations, organized around the fulfilment of societal needs. The family has historically and more or less universally been an integral part of the ethnic community which has promoted patriarchy, especially in the upper income groups. Accordingly, role, power and status are strictly determined by age and gender. Such a patriarchal family does not give equal importance to all individuals in the family. The role of the exclusive earner gives the man the authority to make decisions about his dependents which would mainly include women and children. The family being a closed system, even abuse and violence were allowed in an authoritarian structure.

According to Desai (1993) family laws enacted in India, more or less reflect the traditional norms of families. The family is more open as a system today. Education and modernization have brought importance to the individuals in the family. The family is, therefore, going through a transition from an institution which mainly served the needs of society, to a unit which meets the needs of its members. At present, both the elements coexist in the family to a lesser or greater extent. Lakshminarayana (1982) also stated that today with the advent of diversified occupations and a monetized economy the members in the joint family tend to seek their fortune outside. This change from collective orientation to self-orientation has created problems of adjustment among members in the joint family. Family laws are also undergoing reforms. The family in transition sometimes presents neither traditional norms nor democratic ideals. The growth of individualism has led to the break up of the family system in the developed countries.

The growth of industrialization and technological development have brought several changes in the traditional family all over the world. The urban employment structure has led and is still leading to migration of individuals and families from simple rural living to complex urban centres, weakening their close ties with the family and the community (Desai, 1993).

Education by the family is not adequate at present and training in family occupation is no more necessary. The new work structure has segregated work areas from homes. It has increased the gap between men's roles and women's roles. The status of the elderly as a repository of experiential wisdom is diminishing. The problem of building a career and improving their material conditions keep the earners too preoccupied to think of dependents such as the aged, the disabled, the ill, the unemployed, the widows and so on.

Moreover, the parents academic and career aspirations for their children is motivating them to send their children to pursue their education outside their homes. This deprives the children from their training in familial tasks and their peer group provide them with a different picture of life which may lead to their alienation to their families. This may further lead to problems in adjustment within the family.

In the absence of strong family support, there are increasing number of single-parent families and female headed households. Single parent families are generally headed by women who may be widowed, divorced, separated or deserted. Female heads of households, who are not single parents, may have a migrant husband, or he may not be earning due to disability, unemployment or alcoholism, or he may not be contributing his income to the family. These women have the main earning responsibility when they are neither trained nor experienced to work in the modern economy. Moreover, they have young children to look after. These families are generally the poorest of the poor in any country and need state support. Environmental disasters and political violence have further endangered family life and increased the number of uprooted and refugee families.

Deprivation of families' needs for housing, health, education and income may affect the physical and mental development and the health of individual members, leading to problems such as disability, chronic/terminal illness, substance abuse and so on. In extreme situations, it may lead to the break up of families and destitution of individuals. According to Zimmerman (1989), the relationship between family and environment requires that outputs in the form of governmental policies contribute to environmental stability and prevent family disequilibrium and breakdown. When the family and/or its environment cannot adapt to each other, there exists a state of disequilibrium between the two. The family is vulnerable to disequilibrium not only because of changes internally induced by members and its own development process but because of inputs from the external environment as well (Zimmerman, 1989).

The United Nations has always viewed the institution of the family as the basic unit of the society and has declared 1994 as the International Year of the Family in order to ensure its effective support and empowerment. The major concerns of this step are to support families as basic units, to gain and promote an accurate understanding of family issue to initiate and execute activities to address these issues, particularly at the local and national levels, and to create institutional capabilities of implementating changes at all levels which strengthen the family.

The year also provides us opportunity to reflect upon the needed social policy as may ensure peace and prosperity of the society. The current concern is to make the family as recipient and dispenser of services to involve the family in the resolution of the problems of the individuals so as to establish harmony between the societal control and individual rights (Bedi, 1995).

The review of various studies reveal that the Indian family system has changed its structure from joint to nuclear. This change has occurred due to the operation of the factors, viz., education, modernization, employment opportunities, legislative measures pertaining to land holding and women's rights. The Indian family joint or nuclear is in a state of transition from kin-oriented to an interest oriented family (Lakshminarayana, 1982). The individuals due to alienation from their own families (for various reasons) are in need of education in familial tasks to perform their roles effectively later in life. This is also essential for survival of family as a system.

Conceptual Issues on Women and Family

Transition of family system has brought about change in the women's roles and responsibilities within the families. This in turn has necessitated promotion of FLE to adolescents.

Women have been regarded as the nuclei of a nation. Just as the body is made up of millions of cells controlled by their nuclei, a nation is made up of millions of families depending on the women—housewives and mothers—for their progress and well being. The health and growth of the body of the nation depends on the vitality of its women. Understandably therefore, as the perennial strength of the nation, the women must appreciate their position as also their obligation towards nation building along with the know-how to do-how to fulfil this obligation (Kapoor, 1986).

The Indian women in the family play multiple roles. Primarily, her duties centre around her life in the home and in the labour force. As a home maker, woman is a 24 hour multipurpose worker. Mahatma Gandhi had stated that "Women by nature are intended to be soft, tender-hearted and sympathetic mothers to their children". He had also cautioned women that domestic work output should not take the whole of their time.

Woman is the mother of the race and is the liaison between generations. Nehru once said "To awaken people it is the woman who must be awakened. Once she is on the move, the family moves, the village moves, the nation moves" (Desai, 1967).

In everyday life and in various crisis, woman displays strength and patience in carrying out her responsibilities. Through her hard work and dedication to house keeping, child-rearing and assisting in agriculture and industry, woman contributes much to national, economic and social development. She is responsible for the food the family consumes and for the care of her children. She takes care of food production, food processing, food preparation and serving, cleaning the household, carrying water, gathering fuel and washing dishes and clothes. Management of resources—human and material—sending children to school, meeting the needs of adolescents, improving the environment and planning for her daughter's future are also among her heavy responsibilities. She exerts great influence on the mental and social development of children. Woman is the fulcrum around whom all the decisions and actions of the family revolve (Rajammal, 1985).

According to Lakshmi Devi (1988) "From the time immemorial, women played different roles in their home activities, as wives—in their personal lives with their husbands; as mothers—in their responsibilities for the development of their children; and as home makers—incharge of the operation of their homes. In addition, women also played a pivotal role in agriculture and livestock management.

World conference on Agrarian Reform and Rural Development (WCARRD, 1970) observed that the situation of rural women has been identified as one of the critical manifestations of the growing imbalances, which constitutes a threat not merely to the development of the female population, but to the socio-economic progress of the nations themselves. The maximization of output in growth models, particularly in maximization of food production, the need to contain human misery, malnutrition and hunger that interfere with productivity and growth and above all the need to reduce the rate of population growth are all linked up with better understanding of the situation of women. Since, the largest section of women in the world live in rural areas, and in the Third World countries, the majority of them are engaged in agricultural production, processing and distribution of products, the issue of rural women's participation in development, the manner in which their position and roles are being affected by the process of change call for a far more critical analysis and understanding than they have received in the past developmental strategies.

The National Institute of Rural Development and F.A.O workshop on the integration of women in agriculture and rural development (1980) observed that there is an urgent need to expand knowledge and statistical data on all aspects of the rural poor, particularly with regard to women's role in the society.

Several studies have indicated that women play a significant role in the development of families. Women's health, nutritional status, educational level and earning capacity were found to influence the quality of family life.

A country's future lies in the hands of its women. Because it is the women who give birth to and look after children. Children are the future citizens of India. If they are to be born healthy and looked after well enough to grow up to be strong and useful citizens, then their mothers have to be strong and healthy too. Mothers must also know about how to look after their children, how to prevent them from falling ill and what to do if they do fall ill. Mothers must know about all the different things which will help in the proper development of their children (Mathew, 1988). In spite of the various welfare and educational programmes initiated by the government, a large section of Indian women continue to live in almost the same conditions as were faced by their counterparts centuries ago. They are not only unaware of their significance to the family and the nation but are also ignorant of the rapid strides made elsewhere in the sphere concerning quality of family life.

According to the Ministry of Social Welfare (1985), in Indian Society, the position of women has been traditionally that of a dependent—first on parents, then on husbands and later on the sons. The woman assists her mother in her childhood; after marriage, her role is that of wife and mother. The traditional functions of the family are transmission of culture; child care; marriage and family relations, inculcation of religious and spiritual values.

The family is the most important socializing agency. The task of promoting healthy development of child falls on the shoulders of the parents, especially the mother, who provides all atmosphere of acceptance, love and encouragement to set up and strengthen the child's self image. Rural women were found to be more authoritarian in disciplining children. Scolding, threatening and physical punishments were found to be more common methods of disciplining them. Today, mothers feel that a child thrives better on warmth, both mental and physical. They adopt mostly democratic methods of disciplining. Educated mothers are better at adopting positive disciplining techniques.

Traditionally among the Hindus, marriage is generally possible within the framework of the caste system only. The attitude of the educated middle class women has however, started to change and they seem less bound by the constraints laid down by traditional patterns of marriage. There is increasing approval of inter-caste marriages among the educated middle class people. There is more evidence that modern women are more in favour of arranged marriages than they were ten years ago. Although the ideology of romantic love marriage has gained popularity in the Indian society and is regarded as a panacea by many social reformers for freeing Indian Society from the strangle-hold of the caste system. The vast majority of the people, both educated and uneducated continue to conform to the traditional pattern of the arranged marriage.

Child marriage has played havoc with the physical and mental health of Indian girls and the age of marriage for girls has been raised from 15 to 18 years. There is considerable improvement in the age at marriage for girls in the cities and among high class families. However, child marriages still continue to be solemnized in rural areas and in the backward sections of the city population. Education of women has tended to raise the age at marriage and lower the birth rate.

Although educational and occupational opportunities are providing women with new roles outside the home, their social position in the family remains largely unchanged because the system of arranged marriage conforms to the authority of caste norms, and the obligation of conformity to the traditional image of woman as wife and mother.

Further Singh's (1994) statement rightly describes the status of women in the modern day as "The Technological advancement has brought a new mode of work relationship in which women find themselves increasingly alienated and suffer a loss of status.

Conceptual Issues on Adolescents and Family Life Education

The need for introducing FLE at adolescence was presented by highlighting the characteristics, developmental tasks and problems of this period of life. Adolescence is a transitional stage between childhood and adulthood. In some ways, adolescents resemble the children they were, yet the many changes they undergo during this stage ensure that they will be different from children in many respects. Similarly, one can see glimpses of the adults, the adolescents will become, but more often it is observed that they do not behave like adults. As adolescents mature, fewer resemblances to children and more similarities to adults are observed.

Adolescents can also be identified by the level of development they have reached in the capabilities and skills needed to function effectively as adults. These developmental tasks include achieving a sense of identity, attaining emotional and financial independence from parents, relating effectively with peers, becoming a sexual person, and choosing and preparing for an occupation (Lloyd, 1985).

Compared to children, adolescents are physically more mature, are more skilled and sophisticated in cognitive abilities have more complex and integrated personalities, and have more effective social skills. These development changes mean that adolescents are capable of taking a more active role in their own development than are children.

Adolescence began to be identified as a separate stage in the life span in the early twentieth century. Early theories of adolescence stressed the biological determinants of behaviour (Hall, 1920; Gesell, 1956; Sigmund, 1920 and Freud, 1937). Later theories emphasized socio-cultural determinants (Sullivan, 1953; Erikson, 1950; Benedict, 1936 and Mead, 1928). More recently, there is a growing awareness of the interaction of biological and social forces, with the emergence, of other view points such as the cognitive, social learning, and development task orientations. No single theory can adequately explain the complexities of adolescent development.

Mahale (1987) defined adolescence as a transition period from childhood to adulthood extending from the eleventh year to the twentieth year, thus encompassing the teenage years.

Boys and girls enter the adolescent years as children and leave them as adults. It is during these years that young people mature and develop the ability to live their lives as autonomous persons. The major thrust of this stage of life is physical maturation. Boys become men and girls attain womanhood during pubescence, with the development of primary and secondary sex characteristics. Kashyap (1993) described the developmental tasks of adolescents as follows :

Acceptance of Changes in Body and Physique

The first and probably the most difficult developmental task for adolescents is the acceptance of their changes in body and physique as well as psychological repercussions. The emergence of adult sexual potency is a source of disturbance and anxiety and may push the young person into clandestine experimentation leading to an increase in promiscuity, teenage pregnancies and venereal disease. Rao (1982) has mentioned studies by Joseph (1973) and Park (1972) which show that the incidence of general disease in youth is on the increase and has begun to constitute a sizable health problem in India too.

Achieving a Satisfying and Socially Accepted Masculine or Feminine Role

A young girl's response to pubertal changes depend upon her attitudes toward herself as a female, and her feeling about her identification figure, the mother, parents are the primary sex role models for their grouping children. Therefore, their understanding of and respect for their own sex roles as well as each other's sex role play an important part in their children imbibing a correct concept of sex roles. Parent's own attitude towards their sex and their child rearing pattern will form the foundation of sex orientation in the life of child. Jay (1983) has cited many case studies where adolescents have had difficulty in sex role identification, and have been driven to immature sexual involvement because of parental attitude and negative portrayal of sexual role by the parents.

Locating Oneself as a Member of One's Generation by Developing More Mature Relations with One's Age Mates

As adolescence is a time for social expansion and development, adolescents tend to centre a great deal of their lives about the activities, interests and attitudes of their peers and the peer groups assume greater importance. The peer culture sets patterns for stacking their claim to adult pleasure of sinuousness. Nearly all adolescents desire acceptance in the eyes of their age-mates and will go to extreme lengths to gain and maintain such acceptance. Hence, selection of friends and extent of interactions with them can be a potential area of family conflict. According to a study by Gangrade (1975), placing greater reliance on peer group was more pronounced in adolescents whose parents were illiterate, conservative or authoritarian. As for mixing with the opposite sex Kashyap (1993) in her study reported that adolescents avoided open clashes with their parents on this issue, but did not care for their parent's opinion when they were out of the house. This behaviour pattern was also observed by Garg and Parikh (1976). Their indepth studies of youth have highlighted the strong ambivalence felt towards peers—the need to differentiate and yet to merge. Their encounters with peers aroused a host of anxieties which generated a sense of significance which had to be coped with before reintegration of self could take place.

Achieving Emotional Independence of Parents

Sociologists and psychologists have viewed adolescence as a key developmental period during which the adolescents seek greater autonomy. Pardeck and Pardeck (1988) were of the view that parenting style, family interaction and transition related to the family life cycle influence the development of autonomy in adolescence. Poole, Sunberg and Tyler (1982), did a comparative study of adolescents' perceptions of family decision making and autonomy in India, Australia and in United States. Their findings show that Indian adolescents reported lesser opportunity for acting autonomously. The father had significantly more say in decision making with both boys and girls in India. Their findings point to the fact that Indian families do not place such a high value on independence and self-reliance, and generally have not trained children for autonomy and responsibility other than obeying their elders and doing their family duty.

Selecting and Preparing for an Occupation and Economic Independence

It is during adolescence that the young persons try to think and aspire towards his/her future career. In the fulfilment of this development task, the family plays an important role, as all the youth's aspirations, values and goals are indirectly influenced by the family situation in which they were moulded during the whole childhood period.

The study by Gangrade (1975), indicated significant difference in the two generations with respect to occupational aspirations. The youth were more inclined towards occupations which offered adventure, challenges and better monetary prospects while parents were more concerned with the security offered by any occupation. According to Mahale (1987), the rural adolescent girl in India is usually illiterate or a school drop out. She is invariably married around the time of puberty and passes on to motherhood and so has no scope to think of economic independence. Majority of the boys in the villages are semi-literate. They hardly have a vocation as they are expected to work with their elders as soon as they are able.

Preparing for Marriage and Family Life

Nearly all marriages in India are arranged marriages, specially in the villages. Selection of the spouse is done by elders in the family and within the same caste or subcaste. Love and self-choice marriages are exceptions. According to Sathe (1987), most girls in rural areas are married around the time of puberty. Again there is a great social and family pressure on the young couple to prove their fertility within a year of marriage. Fertility control is not always left to the choice of the couple since the rearing of children is considered a family responsibility.

According to Mahale's study (1987) of schooling adolescents and their families, the general tendency among parents of all educational levels is that their attitudes toward their daughter's marriage is more conservative than toward their son's marriage. Marriage was a topic least discussed in the family. Gangrade's study (1975) gives a similar findings on the aspect.

Establishing One's Identity as a Socially Responsible Person

A specific unique task of adolescence is the establishment of "ego identity". The family, especially the parents, play a major role in shaping the process. This is a period of strain in most families. As adolescents strive to establish their identity, and to emancipate themselves from their parents, the parents tend to feel that their children under value them—and the adolescents believe that adults generally depreciate teenagers. However, when parents accept themselves as they are, with all their weaknesses and strengths and when they accept their several roles at this stage of development without undue conflict or sensitivity, they set a pattern for a similar sort of self-acceptance in their children.

Experts in family life education agree that the primary responsibility for FLE rest with the parents. Research studies, however, have proved that the vast majority of parents do not accept the responsibility for providing FLE to their adolescent sons and daughters. Adams (1985) reported that schools have increasingly been challenged to accept the responsibility for FLE, as the inadequacy of knowledge among young adolescents and the consequences of their ignorance have drawn public attention. Trivedi (1976) stated that there has been an increasing realization of the necessity for imparting education about family including reproductive biology to adolescents. Psychologists and educationists strongly feel that FLE should form an integral part of the regular school curriculum, as this information helps the adolescents to become emotionally stable and to develop a wholesome character.

According to various studies conducted in 1989, population of adolescents (10-19 years) in India was about 22.5 per cent. The distribution of rural and urban population of adolescents was 78.4 and 21.6 per cent respectively. Several studies have urged that a high priority be given to the adolescent girls health and welfare programmes in order to overcome the problem of low birth weight and improve maternal nutritional status as well as maternal morbidity pattern (NIPCCD, 1990).

For rural girls, end of childhood marks the beginning of adulthood and adolescence has been regarded merely as a brief interlude between puberty and marriage. Studies have indicated discrimination against the girl child especially in the distribution of food in the family. Such pattern of insufficient food combined with early marriage often results in the poor adolescent growth. It has been noted that poor maternal nutrition has adverse effects on the birth weight and infant mortality rates.

Gopalan's study on adolescent girls advocated that public

policy should focus on the health and nutritional status of women. He also stressed the need for education for better living and vocational training for rural adolescent girls.

The Government of India has been making efforts to make adolescent girls, participants of the major development programme, i.e., the Integrated Child Development Services (ICDS). The scheme proposed by the Department of Women and Child Development envisages the inclusion of a programme of upliftment of adolescent girls as part of the total agenda of its ICDS operation. The World Health Assembly had declared a new programme—Adolescent Health into the Eighth General Programme of work of WHO (1990-95). WHO, UNFPA and UNICEF are committed to provide support to such efforts. A review of Governmental and international agency programmes in India indicate that more emphasis is laid on health and nutritional status of adolescents. Inclusion and interweaving of FLE into these programmes may achieve greater benefits and may directly have a bearing on the quality of the future generations.

Adolescents also form the target groups of NAEP. In a wider perspective, NAEP includes literacy, leading to development of new knowledge and skills and hopefully, to a capacity to imbide social change and meet new situations and it has a key role to play far beyond the realm of letters and numbers (Wadia, 1979). The contribution of NAEP to FLE in India is briefly discussed in the following section.

The National Adult Education Programme has been launched with the intention to do something more effective, more speedily in the sphere of adult literacy. Wadia (1979) stated that unlike a pedagogic system, where the student is expected to imbibe new knowledge as a discipline, in the non-formal milieu and particularly where adult illiterates are concerned, the educational materials have to touch life as it is lived, so that they are not only immediately relevant, but preferably a matter of self-interest. Wadia (1979) reiterated that in the case of adults in the reproductive age groups, health, sex and family planning education are a most significant and rewarding part of non-formal education. This does not amount to family planning motivation as such, but can and should provide a valuable information base. NAEP envisaged a special FLE unit as part of population education in structure. A review of NAEP from its inception will be highly helpful in assessing its suitability to impart FLE more effectively and comprehensively.

Conceptual Issues on Non-formal Adult Education Programme (NFAEP)

The concept of adult education is so broad and its purpose is so comprehensive that it does not easily lend itself to a proper or a satisfactory definition. In understanding the concept of adult education, it is relevant to consider the meaning of adult. Adulthood is primarily conceived as one of the stages in the process of human development and growth (Boring *et al.*, 1956). The phase of adulthood, as per the chronological age of the individuals, is perceived differently by various earlier studies. Reviewing the status of adult education, the situation committee (1944) considered persons in the age group of 10-35 years as adults. Based on the Saxena report (1948), the Central Advisory Board of Education in India recommended that adults of the age group of 12 to 45 years are to be imparted adult education. At a subsequent stage, the provincial education officers reduced the upper limit for adult to 40 years. The Education Commission (1964-66) considered people in the age group of 15-45 years as adults for the purpose of adult education, contrary to the earlier understanding, which considered people in the age group of 10 to 45 years as adults. The NAEP aimed at spreading literacy among the 10 crores of illiterate population in the age group of 15 to 35 years in India.

In the opinion of Chandrasekar (1982), the age group 15-35 years is the most productive group with a substantial proportion of illiterate population. While there was a considerable debate on the age differentials for considering a person as adult in the literacy programmes in India, the third international conference on Adult Education sponsored by UNESCO deleted importance to the age of the individual and recommended that a person needs adult education provided he is a drop out or an illiterate. Thus for generic purpose adult education aims at imparting education for the illiterate or dropout and specifically for those who are in the age group 15-35 years.

The concept of education is generally misconceived as equivalent to literacy. Literacy is conceived only as one of the areas of education and more specifically a tool to promote education. In reality, education is the process through which the faculty of reasoning is developed among the human beings, in order to make them distinguish between right and wrong (Madan, 1978). Accordingly, UNESCO has listed the following goals for education:

- education enables the mankind to live a fuller, meaningful and happier life;
- education develops the best elements in the human culture;
- education aims at promoting social and economic well being of the people; and
- the ultimate objective of education is to enable the mankind to lead a happy life (Gray, 1956).

The concept of adult education is educating the adult in all those programmes which aims at educating the adult illiterates. Stressing this, Ranjan (1967) describes adult education as—"the most common and universally used form of expression to those who at their educable age could not or did not go in for formal schooling".

Similar views on adult education were expressed by Liveright and Maygood (1968) for whom adult education is "a process whereby persons, who no longer (or did not) attend school on a regular and full-time basis undertake sequential and organized activities with a conscious intention of bringing about changes in information, knowledge, understanding or skills, appreciation and attitudes or for the purpose of identifying and solving personal or community problems".

The felt needs of adult learners become the real needs for the formation of adult education programme. Walker and Kumar (1988) has rightly pointed out that "Philosophical theories have little conscious effect upon the hundreds of thousands of learning activities now being pursued by millions of people" Gandhiji (1939) defined "adult education as education for life, i.e., adult education is not just that which continues throughout life time, but that which is essential for life. Secondly, it is not just for teaching literacy." He further stated that "Though mass illiteracy is India's sin and shame, the literacy campaign must not begin and end with mere knowledge of the alphabet. It must go hand in hand with the spread of useful knowledge. Adult education in the above context is viewed as a broad concept aiming at the overall development of the community through raising the individual standards in the areas of knowledge, skills and attitudes.

National Adult Education Programme

The number of illiterates in India has been growing constantly an increase of 140 million in 35 years is reported. During the last decade, the increase had been 6 million per year. The educational system, with inadequate school facilities and a programme irrelevant to a vast majority, keeps out almost 70 per cent of the nation's children. Nearly 20 per cent do not go to school at all, 50 per cent of those who go to school quit in the first standard itself, 60 per cent abandon it before the fifth standard (age 11), and 75 per cent before the fifth standard (age 11), and 75 per cent before the eighth standard (age 14). The drop out rate is extremely high. Since three to four years of schooling are required for lasting literacy, the majority who drop out of school relapse into illiteracy (Saraswathi, 1984).

The promise implicit in the Constitution of India that "The State shall endeavour to provide, within a period of 10 years from the commencement of this Constitution, for free and compulsory education for all children until they complete the age of 14 years" remains to be fulfilled.

From the picture presented, it is evident that the system of formal education caters to only a small per cent of the population, ignoring a vast majority. The existing system is perpetuated by promoting the values of competition, inequality and individual self-interest, essentially by focusing on subject matter learning and by measuring success through examination results, with little or no respect given to the learner, his needs, interests and capabilities. In this context, a search for an alternative system is essential. In the past decade, efforts have been made by both governmental and non-governmental organizations to find an alternative. It was in 1978 that the government declared that the highest priority would be accorded to adult education.

In the Sixth Five Year Plan, adult education constituted one of the minimum needs of the poorest sections of society. Now the National Adult Education Programme (NAEP) has become the education imperative of a national effort to provide a fair deal to those in greatest need of it. A well planned specific administrative structure has been set up for NAEP. NAEP has taken shape of mass programme and had been launched to cover 11.50 crores of the illiterate population in the age group 15-35 years by the end of the Seventh Five Year Plan, i.e., by 1990, apart from being a part of the Prime Minister's 20-point Economic Programme.

In emphasizing the correlation between working, living and learning, NAEP has borrowed heavily from Gandini's basic education (Nai Taleem). In its methods, NAEP incorporates the essential feature of non-formal education, particularly emphasizing relevance to the environment and learner's needs, flexibility regarding duration, location of institutional arrangements, etc., and diversification in curriculum and in learning materials.

As NAEP uses non-formal approach, it is more relevant to use the term non-formal adult education (NFAEP) in place of national adult education programme (NAEP). In the present study the terms NFAEP and NAEP were used synonymously.

The adult education programme at present is being implemented through the following schemes :

a.	Rural Function Literacy project	-	Centre sponsored scheme
b.	State Adult Education Programme	-	State sector scheme
c.	Assistance to Voluntary Agencies	-	Central scheme working in the field of Adult Education
d.	UGC-Assisted Adult Education Programme	-	Central Scheme
e.	Mass Programme of Functional Literacy—A voluntary programme being implemented through NSS and non-NSS students from the summer vacations of 1986	-	Centre sponsored scheme
f.	Shramik Vidyapeeths	-	Centre sponsored scheme

National policy on education looks at adult education as an essential part of the strategy to reduce educational disparities and as a means of people's liberation from ignorance and oppression. "The whole nation", NPE declares, "must pledge itself to the eradication of illiteracy, particulary in 15-35 age group". The National policy on Education envisages that programmes of literacy can become meaningful only when they come along with a package comprising practical information and skills relevant to day-to-day needs of learners.

The main features of the adult education programme, as spelt out, in Programme of Action include :

(a) establishing a close linkage between adult education and development programmes,
(b) reorganisation of the existing programmes,
(c) a distinct slant towards women's equality,
(d) harnessing science and technology for improving the environment, content and pace of learning,
(e) launching of mass functional literacy programme,

(f) a multi-dimensional programme of continuing education,
(g) creation of dynamic management structures to cope with the tasks envisaged, etc.

The Programme of Action highlights development of systematic adult education programme linked with national goals such as alleviation of poverty, adoption of small family norm, national integration, environmental conservation, promotion of women equality, etc. The mass literacy programme would include in addition to literacy, functional knowledge and skills, an awareness among learners about the socio-economic realities and the possibility to change it. The policy also envisages participation of all sections of society indicative of their commitment to eradication of illiteracy to make it a truly national programme (DAE, 1988).

Administrative Structure of Adult Education

The personnel system is of great importance to any programme. The success of a programme depends upon a well equipped and properly oriented personnel system. This is more so in the context of a programme which is to act as an agent of directed and rapid socio-economic transformation (Kumar, 1988).

The step wise description of the administrative set up of the NAEP is as follows :

At the national level, the National Directorate of Adult Education (NDAE) is at the apex of the administrative setup. It is the apex executive, and monitoring body of the structure. The Director, a few deputy Directors and a vast supporting staff constitute this body. It is an allied wing of the Education Department of the Government of India.

NDAE established in 1977, is headed by the Minister of Human Resources Development of the Government of India with the Ministers of Agriculture and Rural Development, Labour, Health and Family Planning and Information and Broadcasting, the Ministers of Education from different states, certain officials and nine eminent non-officials with experience and expertise in the field of education as members. The Board has set up the following committees to attend to specific tasks, namely, Committees on (a) Preparatory action; (b) motivation; (c) voluntary agencies; (d) post literacy and follow up programmes; and (e) evaluation.

During the First and Second Year Plan (1951-61)

administrative structures at the state and district levels were created with considerable care and imagination. Each state has a State Directorate of Adult Education (SDAE) with adequate staff and facilities. In a few states, these directorates form part of the directorates of school education.

State Board of Adult Education (SBAE) is headed by the Chief Minister or the Education Minister of the state and includes the ministers responsible for the major development programmes. The board also includes heads of developmental departments, representatives of universities, industrial establishments, voluntary agencies, adult education experts, social workers, and persons belonging to the Scheduled Castes and the Scheduled Tribes as members. The Board is thus a 'comprehensive consortium'.

For the success of any programme, a strong resource base is required. In the field of adult education, the National Directorate of Adult Education has been functioning as the National resource agency. Since the main responsibility for the implementation of the NAEP is on the state governments. State resource centres (SRC) have been set up in different states to support the programme with required technical assistance in different fields. SRC is mainly responsible for preparation of education materials, monitoring and evaluation of NAEP at state level.

In the district administrative system, the head of NAEP is the district Collector. Each district is also provided with a district adult education officer (DAEO) assisted by some supervisory staff. Every district has District Adult Education Board (DAEB) entrusted with the responsibility of co-ordinating and overseeing the programme. In every district there is a purchase committee for the purpose of marketing and purchase of necessary equipment.

One of the most important innovations introduced in the NFAEP is the project approach. The project is critical at the field level in the administrative and planning processes of the NAEP. The minimum desirable number of adult education centres in one project was assumed to be 100 and the maximum 300. Thus, if an area contains 900 illiterate adults of the age group 15-35, that area will be considered as a project area.

The staffing pattern for the projects has been worked out keeping in view the role and responsibilities of the project. The project is headed by a senior level Project Officer (P.O.) assisted by an Assistant Project Officer (A.P.O.) if the size of the project is large. In addition, an A.P.O. is envisaged for post literacy and follow-up activities. Each project has a project Adult Education Advisory

Committee. The supervisors at project level serve as the link between the project office and adult education centres.

At village level/community level animators/instructors are responsible for the NAEP. Each Adult Education Centre (AEC) comprises 30 learners. The number of AEC in a village/area depends upon the number of illiterates therein. Adult Education Centres exclusively for women have been started, to promote adult education among women.

The principal objectives of the programme relate to :

- increasing the awareness of the people about themselves and about the social reality around them;
- organizing them;
- assisting them to understand and solve their problems;
- involving them in meaningful and challenging tasks of social and national development; and
- helping the individual learner to solve his personal problems.

The conceptual frame of NAEP has been concretized by emphasizing the following three aspects of the content.

Literacy and Numeracy

Of a sufficient level to enable the learners to continue self-reliant learning.

Functional Development

Functionality viewed as the role of the individual as a producer, worker, a member of the family and as a citizen in a civic and political system.

Social Awareness

Including an awareness about the impediments to development, about laws and government policies, and the need for the poor and illiterate to organise themselves in pursuit of their legitimate interests and for group action. The conceptual position of the NAEP, however, extend well beyond these elements (Anil, 1982).

In the place of centre based adult education centres, Total Literacy Campaign was launched in the year 1990 in all the districts of the State of Andhra Pradesh. The campaign mobilises students and non-students to participate in the programme voluntarily (Zilla Saksharata Samithi).

Curriculum for National adult education has to be flexible in timing, duration, place, content, method and media, and the instruction and it cannot be rigid. It should be based on their interests, needs and problems, as needs and interests are changing, curriculum has to respond to those changing needs. Curriculum of NAEP must address to a definite specific target group such as men, women, urban and rural people as the needs of each group differs. Curriculum development should be a participatory process. To be effective, it needs the support of all concerned and is not one man's job. It should be a joint, co-operative and collaborative effort of a team of personnel involved in such programmes (Manii, 1989).

The curriculum designed for the learners should enable them to solve their familial, economic, ecological, social and environmental problems. Hence, the participation of the learners is essential and they should be consulted well before the design of the curriculum. Such a need-based, problem-oriented and functionally related approach directly implies that neither diversification and environment are identical in structure and characteristics, nor are the attitudes, approaches, interests, needs and responses of adults in different situations are uniform.

The impact of AEP on women's lives is an under researched area. Research evidence is still not available on the overall impact of various literacy programmes on women. Women have a different pace and rhythm of learning. They take interest in learning when it relates to their daily life. Literacy primers and related materials would therefore need to be carefully designed. Since the dominant language of literacy reproduces patriarchal ideology and legitimises popular knowledge of poor illiterate, special efforts must be made to provide opportunities for creative expression in popular forms such as stories, songs, plays, etc., that women seem comfortable with.

The experience of Mathur (1989) found that females who were exposed to adult education programmes for five years have displayed significantly better and favourable attitudes toward family planning, better home adjustment and a higher level of social awareness. A new need based NAEP curriculum can sensitise the adolescent girls to their family conditions and will help them to widen their vision of themselves and to see their own individual and family circumstances in the light of the knowledge gained and act in accordance. NAEP curriculum highlights home and family life as one of its content (Wadia, 1979). A FLE curriculum based on perceived needs of experts and learners, if implemented through NAEP could reach the unreached youth and can make a new level of human awareness and quality of life.

Family Life Education in India : A Historical Review

The process of education for family living is probably as old as life, and built into its very existence. Up to recent times, individuals in different societies learnt skills for family living informally. The sources for such learning available in this country were many. The major source as in any other country was, and even today remains, the first hand experience of living and interacting in families, and observing others. Some other sources in India included people, socio-religious and cultural customs, and selected life practices.

Among the people who got involved with family life education were (i) the older relatives and family friends who gave advice to the younger members of the family, based on the wisdom acquired through their own life experiences and analytical observation of others going through the various stages of life and events; (ii) the peer group who shared life experiences and (iii) the preachers who cited scriptures and other literary work to emulate roles.

Socio-religious customs that encouraged attitudes towards family members were handed down from one generation to another. In addition, festivals, folklore and songs gave the cultural tone and added humour to daily living. These contributed to some understanding of the dynamics, role content, adjustment and stress management.

Selected life practices, based on knowledge accumulated over centuries, were handed down to give opportunities to relax, reflect and gain some self awareness and control. Some of these sources, as agents of informal preparation for family living, still continue to make their impact. However, the impact of the various societal changes in the last few decades is reflected in the individual's expectations and acceptance as he/she carries out the role in the family. Since these expectations and acceptance of norms have changed, intervention is required to help the family achieve this transition by retaining what is meaningful, discarding what is not, and incorporating what may be new and useful (Gokarn, 1986).

Family Life Education (FLE), which relates to a wide range of issues at the familial level, it has emerged as a discipline drawing information from various disciplines and experiences, viz., population education, home science, social work, adult education and women's development studies.

The pioneering work in the area of FLE was done by Family Planning Association of India (FPAI), a national voluntary organisation which was founded in 1949 in Bombay. The organization is devoted to promoting knowledge of family planning as a basic human right as well as population policies which can help bring about a balanced development of the resources of the country—both human and material—as a means towards raising the quality of life.

In the year 1951, the Government of India sponsored a National Family Planning Programme to reduce population. The programme was later merged with material and child health services as family planning programme revolved around the mother and the child. Further, this integrated approach was also strengthened by the All India Post Partum Programme in the year 1967 to promote contraceptive acceptance among women coming to Government hospitals for delivery or abortion (Wadia, 1987).

National Family Planning Programme received a serious set back due to mass sterilization camps in 1970. In an attempt to tone down the reaction to the excesses in the family planning programme, it was renamed as 'Family Welfare Programme' wherein family planning has been perceived as 'an integral part of comprehensive policy covering education, health, maternity and child care, family welfare, women's rights and nutrition'. Massive educational and motivational drives have been launched to promote the programme (Ministry of Health and Family Welfare, 1978).

The population issue which so closely influences quality of human life and which ultimately is controlled by personal family decision making, within the closed family, is the important reason for integrating family life related issues with population education.

The concepts of population education and family life education have natural and logical linkages with each other. They represent two dimensions of people's lives and life issues in the contemporary world. The focus of population education is the aggregate formulations of the broader population environment dynamics operating within the total developmental perspective.

In the scheme of these interactions, the individual and the family, occupy an important logical and structural position. The features that are reflected in the population are the results of actions and events that take place at the family level. Population characteristics such as size, distribution, age structure, sex ratio, events such as marriage, birth, death, migration, qualitative components in terms of health, wealth, education, food, employment, social welfare, social justice, human dignity, human rights and inter-personal relations all have their reflections at the micro level. For instance, large population is a reflection of larger families in the context of the level of socio-cultural and economic development of a given society. The concept of family in population links the demographic with the socio-cultural and psychological aspects of human matters. Population thus relates to people while family relates to persons. The efforts in both postulates are towards the improvement of human conditions and integration and enrichment of human life inclusive of the improvement and preservation of the total environment (Merh, 1984).

The expressions 'Population Education' (PE) and 'Family Life Education' (FLE) have been used interchangeably and flexibly in developing a variety of programmes. A synoptic review of population education literature since its inception in 1969 to date bears out this fact. In programmes that are being formulated in recent years whenever the point of reference in family education, an effort is made to encompass the ecological, social and developmental aspects as they relate to family matters. Even though conceptual clarity with regard to this educational area is gradually emerging due to inadequate information and data, absence of scientific and qualitative indications, lack of integration of knowledge base pertaining to the specifics of our own Indian situations has showed its progress.

FLE is perceived to be usually operating through informal channels, education which incidentally everyone receives. Many programmes have been conceived and implemented in India for extension education of women. Notably, family life education was an important constituent of most of them. Their objectives have been defined and accordingly, their contents have been conceptualised. In actual implementation, no programme provides family life education, except Grihini Training Programme. Grihini training programmes are intended for tribal girls in Bihar, Madhya Pradesh, West Bengal, Orissa and Maharashtra (Kapoor, 1986).

The factors responsible for the activities of family life education not being conducted in the spirit and to the extent they should be, were revealed in a study conducted by Kapoor (1986). The factors are three fold; first, the factors that relate to the physical facilities available in the centres; second, those that pertain to the field level functionaries and third, those that concern the supervision and guidance given to field level functionaries. This indicates that there is a great need to reinforce and strengthen the existing extension education programmes in order to impart family life education to the needy groups.

Population and family life related issues were not considered to be within the purview of the subject of home science until recently. A survey of home science colleges and their involvement in family planning and population education related activities (Verma, 1980) indicated that it has been a common practice to involve a doctor or public health person to give lectures on specific topic, i.e., contraception or family planning methods, etc., included in courses such as marriage and family relations, adolescent development, which are taught in home science colleges. In 1971, the American Home Economics Association (AHEA) brought together a group of international home economists to discuss the need for home economists around the world to actively involve themselves in programmes dealing with family planning, population education and quality of life of individuals and families. In 1974, the international family planning project of American Home Economics Association and the International Planned Parenthood Federation (IPPF) were launched and a series of workshops, seminars and summer institutes were organized with the objective of bringing about greater involvement of home economists in this field. The field of home science focuses on the family, its dynamics and the inter relationship within it; it aims at promoting the quality of life of individuals and families in the communities.

Though some sporadic efforts have been made in India by various organizations/academic institutions to impart family life education to needy groups, not many programmes had been planned and organized on the basis of scientific research.

Family Life Education : Concept and Need

Family Life Education (FLE) in its broadest sense, includes all formal educational efforts designed to prepare people at any stage to make the most of family living. A well integrated programme of FLE could help families adopt themselves to new changes, and assume greater responsibility for the transformation of society. According to Smith (1976), Family Life Education is a programme of learning experiences, structured to develop the potentials of family members, to play their present and future roles. Its central concept is that of relationships through which the personality develops, individuals make decisions and gain the convictions of self worth. FLE is a strategy to enrich family life through effective and efficient programmes. It consists of planned intervention methods to help improve the quality of individuals and their family living (Balu, 1989).

FLE as a formally structured intervention to help members of the family, has been practiced for over a few decades. Yet even today, what FLE is and what it ought to be, remains the subject of a continuing debate. It is, however, accepted that the FLE approach is both preventive and developmental, and is directed 'to teach' people to 'live together', creatively and with affection in the family. With respect to the theoretical under pinnings of the FLE, there is no fully accepted single frame of reference. Hence, any frame considered should be viewed as open and liable to additions and modifications. Such a situation is not uncommon in a growing profession where practice develops theory as much as guiding the practice. Theory building is a continuous process, and therefore, framing some outline and viewing it as permanent would be defeating the very process of theory building.

Currently, FLE is described as "A programme of learning experiences planned and guided to develop the potential of individuals in their present and future roles as family members" (Smith, 1976). This description of FLE by Smith was adopted by him from Avery's (1962) definition. Most family life educators wholly accept this statement and add further dimensions to it.

The National Council of Family Relations of America (NCFRA), stated that FLE is intended "To guide individuals and families in improving their interpersonal relationships and furthering their maximum development". In addition, the Council stated that FLE programmes "seek to improve their quality of life throughout the entire range of human development". The range includes physical and emotional growth, individual and sexual development, dating and courtship, marriage and parenthood". It continuously emphasizes the importance of personal, integrity and family responsibility (Smith, 1970). However, some extra dimensions are added to the range described above such as, the physical, socio-psychological growth and sexual development, pre-marriage preparation, marriage, parenthood, in-law relationship, grand-parenthood and spirituality of the members of the family. India being a technologically developing country, areas such as environmental and personal hygiene, preventive health and nutrition are to be woven into the programme content (Gokarn 1986).

Family Life Education is not to be confused with sex education, for it is much broader in scope, though sex education, is a part of it. The complexity of today's cultural milieu, the multiplicity of forces working upon the individual, the widening intergenerational gaps require an educational approach which is likely to help different members of the family to asses his or her role to create a harmony and strength in the family unit. Consequently family life education needs to be imparted at different levels, by different agents to different members of the family and the society. There is a need to strengthen and renew this basic unit and nucleus of the society in view of the rapid change.

In order to plan a need based FLE programme for different target groups, it becomes necessary to explore the existing needs and knowledge of individuals for whom the programme is being made. This would provide a baseline data for planning and developing the curriculum (Acchpal and Verma, 1988). Thus, a series of researches were undertaken to meet this endeavour. The first research was undertaken by Karnick (1978) and Dave (1982) who studied the knowledge content of secondary school boys and girls from Udaipur district, which further led to the formulation of a need based curriculum on population education for secondary school boys and girls by Dave (1982). Similarly, another study was conducted by Dhar (1981) who initially studied the knowledge content of non-school going adolescent girls residing in a slum community of Baroda in order to develop a "learning package" on family life education, for the out of school adolescent girls. Roongruang (1983) also studied knowledge content of boys and girls in Thailand on population issues with similar objectives.

Viewing the results of Karnick's (1978) and Dave's (1982) investigations, it was observed that most secondary school boys and girls possessed more than 50 per cent knowledge on various population issues, namely: demography (49.5 %), human reproduction (53.96 %), determinants and consequences of population growth (51.53 %) and family planning (56.85 %). Comparison of percentage responses showed that the secondary school students lacked knowledge mainly in the area of demography and determinants and consequences of population control.

In a study on knowledge content of secondary school boys and girls in Thailand, Roongruang (1983) reported a higher per cent of knowledge content amongst boys and girls making an aggregate of 72.79 per cent on almost all population issues. Results showed that the knowledge content of the sample in Thailand was higher (72.29 %) than that of India (52.90 %) and thus incorrect responses were given by 26.54 and 46.53 per cent of the Thai and Indian sample respondents respectively.

Knowledge content on non-school going adolescent girls from a community in Baroda in a study conducted by Dhar (1982) also indicated low per cent of knowledge content in all areas of population and family life related issues. Most of the girls indicated a low understanding in the area of determinants and consequences of population growth, decision making, economic considerations and nutrition.

Karnick (1978), Dave (1981) and Roongruang (1983) revealed some interesting findings. The first two studies revealed that girls had more knowledge content in all the issues related to population except on demography though this difference was not very significantly marked. Comparison of the percentages of correct responses by girls and boys also revealed that boys had more knowledge content in the area of demography, and determinants and consequences of population growth as compared to the other two areas, i.e., human reproduction and family planning where the girls scored higher.

Further, the foregoing studies indicated that though school and non-school going boys and girls had some knowledge of the various population issues, a detailed analysis of the statements under each major issue showed that there were still some essential gaps in their knowledge which were necessary to be eliminated through an educational programme in population and family life related issues.

The Family Planning Association of India (FPAI) has done pioneering work in the field of population, sex and family life education. FPAI (1990) in their study found that 96.30 per cent of the principals, 97.0 per cent of the teachers, 89.3 per cent of the parents, 99.9 per cent of the boys and 81.8 per cent of the girls felt that there was definite need for the introduction of family life education at the secondary school level.

The study further revealed that only 5-10 per cent of the girls in the formal sector attended FLE course when it was offered on a voluntary basis for both boys and girls. However, when it was conducted exclusively for girls the response was remarkably better. In the same study, majority of the respondents argued that 14-15 was the best age to start family life education for boys and 12-13 years for girls.

In another study of FPAI, the boy students expressed equal preference for doctors (39.8 per cent) and volunteer teachers (35.6 per cent) to teach them family life education. While, the girl students expressed first preference to volunteer teachers (51.1 per cent) and last preference to doctors (23.0 per cent). About half of the parents (49.2 per cent) expressed their disinclination to undertake the responsibility for giving family life knowledge to young people, while 46.3 per cent were willing to do, provided they have received some special training in it (FPAI, 1990).

The effort to provide FLE for young people, both in school and out of school has been receiving attention in recent years. For example, Singh (1979) stressed the need for exposing both student and non-student youth to population education so as to enable them to understand how a fast growing population can effect the quality of life. In developing countries the youth non-student present a tremendous challenge and the study has failed to suggest a methodology to promote FLE among this group.

Mere reliance on formal education cannot cover all the educational needs in India. Since population education is not necessarily of educating the unaffected, unorganized youth, who are not reached by conventional school programmes should receive importance (Zaveri, 1979). This is the only means by which youth in different settings with different levels of understanding could be reached (Shah, 1980). But the content and method of delivery of the non-formal education, however, remains unclear.

Major Observations

The available literature on FLE was reviewed and the gaps in the literature were identified.

The universal significance of family as a social institution was highlighted through concepts, meanings, definitions by various experts, which stressed that the joint family in India has provided economic, social and emotional support to its members. The head of the family commands respect and authority over the family that is children and grand children. Any member who is in difficulty, can fall back upon the family, get shelter, advice and take moral support. Family is portrayed as a fountain of love, affection and security for its members.

Further, the family is viewed (Kulkarni, 1977) as a link between continuity and change. Besides the individual and the community, it is the family which provides a third dimension of depth to the evolution of mankind. The family is also conceived as "A unit of interacting personalities (Schvaneu *et al.*, 1966). As the family is a system of inter-dependent and reciprocal relationships, the behaviour of any family members affects all others in the family (Kashyap, 1993).

Based on the United Nations Report on Human rights (1987), Desai (1993) applied human rights to the family at three levels and they are:

- the individuals rights to have a family;
- the individuals rights within the family;
- the family's rights with reference to its environment.

The studies on the nature, patterns and types of Indian families reveal the following—A family is a group of people who generally live under one roof, who eat food cooked in one kitchen, who hold property in common, participate in common family worship and are related to one another..." (Karve, 1968).

The fundamental characteristic of traditional Hindu Family is its joint nature. Besides being joint in structure, the Hindu Family has been patriarchal, patrilineal, patrilocal and monogamous in nature. The possibility of matrilocal joint families cannot be completely ruled out but such cases are quite exceptional. Thus it can be said that in the Hindu Society the traditionally approved family form has been patriarchal joint family system (Sahay, 1969).

The traditional Indian family which has been characterized as joint family must have emerged as early as the vedic period in an agrarian society based on plough cultivation. This then was an ideal setting for an institution like joint family with its emphasis on common living. But the circumstances under which the institution flourished in traditional Hindu Society could not ever remain the same. The traditional Hindu family lost its natural base and is faced with the problem of survival (Parmar, 1987). In contrast to this Desai (1994) stated that family studies in India have always been on whether joint family is breaking down as a result of industrialisation and urbanisation. When the joint family system was prevalent only among minority of the population, and when urbanism existed in India prior to industrialisation, the question whether industrialisation and urbanisation have led to its break up is out of place.

Socio-economic development based on the western model, has brought positive and negative effects on the Indian families, especially in the roles and responsibilities of family members, the educational and occupational opportunities are providing women with new roles outside the home, their social position in the family remained largely unchanged because the system of arranged marriage confirms the authority of caste norms, and the obligation of conformity to the traditional image of woman as wife and mother. Further, Singh (1994) rightly describes the status of women in the modern day as The technological advancement has brought a new mode of work relationship in which women find themselves alienated and suffer a loss of status.

Several authors opined that industrialisation, urbanisation which brought with it modern education, technology, institution of working women resulting in rural, urban and town metropolitan migration, adversely affected the integrity of joint family. Laws concerning marriage, divorce, inheritance, maintenance, adoption and family, process of development along with the poverty had also positive and negative effects on the status of family. Further the fast changing socio-economic environments and social values, traditional joint family is values, traditional joint family is undergoing a change; the degree of change varying from rural to urban, urban to metropolitan, poverty to affluence, etc., with these demographic changes, the demographic people of the family has also undergone changes.

The demographic and structural changes in the Indian family system, women's employment, class and caste conflict, terrorism and increasing crime rate now left the family members vulnerable to outside and aggression is considered by various experts. In this situation a well integrated programme of FLE could help families adopt themselves to new changes and assume greater responsibility for the transformation of society. According to Smith (1976), FLE is a programme of learning experiences, structured to develop the potentials of family members, to play their present and future roles. Balu (1989) viewed FLE as a formally structured intervention to help members of the family, which has been practiced for over a few decades. Yet even today, what FLE is and what it ought to be, remains the subject of a continuing debate. It is however, accepted that the FLE approach is both preventive and developmental, and is directed 'to team' people to 'live together', creatively and with affection in the family.

Acchpal and Verma (1988), stated that FLE programme has to be planned based on the FLE needs of different target groups. The studies of Karnick (1978) and Dave (1981), revealed that most secondary school boys and girls possessed more than 50 per cent knowledge on various population issues. Doon (1983) reported that the knowledge content of secondary school boys and girls in Thailand was higher than that of India. Dhar (1982), also found that the knowledge content of non-school going adolescent girls in all areas of population and family life related issues was low. The knowledge of FPAI study conducted in 1990, revealed that 96.30 per cent of the principals, 97.6 per cent of the teachers, 89.3 per cent of the parents, 99.9 per cent of the boys and 81.8 per cent of the girls expressed the need for FLE. The study further revealed that only 5-10 per cent of the girls in the formal sector attended FLE course when it was offered on a voluntary basis for both boys and girls. However, when it was conducted exclusively to girls the response was remarkably better. In the same study, majority of the respondents argued that 14-15 years was best age to start FLE to boys and 12-13 years for girls.

A historical review of FLE in India revealed that the process of education for family living was as old as life and was built into its very existence up to recent times. Individuals in different societies learnt skills for family living informally. The sources for such learning in this country varied, viz., the first hand experience of living, observations of others advice from the older relatives and family friends, the peer group and the preachers. According to Gokan (1980) various changes in the society during the last few decades reflected changes in the individuals' expectations and acceptance within the family, intervention is required to help the family achieve this transition by retaining what is meaningful, discarding what is not, and incorporating what may be new and useful.

FLE which relates to a wide range of issues in our lives at the familial level, has emerged as a discipline. FPAI, a national voluntary organization which was founded in 1949 in Bombay, has carried out pioneering work in the area of FLE. Earlier FLE was a component of population education. Merh (1984) stated that the concepts of population education and FLE have natural and logical linkages with each other. They represent two dimensions of people's lives and life issues in the contemporary world.

FLE was a constituent of many extension education programmes implemented in India. Though their objectives and contents have been conceptualised accordingly, in actual implementation, no programme provides FLE, except 'Grihini Training Programmes' of Bihar, Madhya Pradesh, West Bengal, Orissa and Maharashtra, which were intended for tribal girls (Kapoor 1986). The author further stressed the need to reinforce and strengthen the existing extension education programmes in order to impart FLE to needy groups.

According to Verma (1980), population and family life related issues were not considered to be within the purview of home science until recently. In 1971, the American Home Economics Association (AHEA) brought together a group of International Home Economists to discuss the need for home economists around the world to actively involve themselves in programmes dealing with family planning, population education and quality of life of individuals and families. In 1974, the International family project of American Home Economics Association and the International Planned Parenthood Federation (IPPF) were formed and a series of workshops, seminars and summer institutes were organized with the objective of bringing about greater involvement of home economists in the field. The field of home science focuses on the family, its dynamics, and promoting the quality of life of individuals and families in the communities.

Though some sporadic efforts have been made in India by various organizations/academic institutions to impart FLE to groups, not many programmes had been planned and organized on the basis of scientific research. FPAI studies revealed that adolescence is the right age for introduction of FLE.

Adolescence began to be identified as a separate stage in the life span in the early twentieth century. Early theories of adolescence stressed the biological determinants of behaviour (Hall, 1920; Gesell, 1956; Sigmund, 1920 and Freud, 1937). Later theories emphasized social-cultural determinants (Sullivan, 1953; Erikson, 1950; Benedict, 1936 and Mead, 1928). More recently, there is a growing awareness of the interaction of biological and social forces, with the emergencies, of other view points such as the cognitive, social learning, and development task orientations. No single theory can adequately explain the complexities of adolescent development.

Compared to children, adolescents are physically more mature, more skilled and sophisticated in cognitive abilities, have more complex and integrated personalities, and have more effective social skills. These development changes mean that adolescents are capable of taking a more active role in their own development than are children.

Mohale (1987) defined adolescence as a transition period from childhood to adulthood extending from the eleventh year to the twentieth year. Kashyap (1993) described the developmental tasks under the following headings :

- Acceptance of changes in body and physique.
- Achieving a satisfying and socially accepted masculine (or) feminine role.
- Locating oneself as a member of one's own generation by developing more mature relations with one's age mates.
- Achieving emotional independence of parents and other studies.
- Selecting and preparing for an occupation and economic independence.
- Preparing for marriage and family life.
- Establishing one's identity as a socially responsible person.

These developmental tasks need to be completed without undue conflict or sensitivity, only then they set a pattern for a similar sort of self-acceptance in their children.

Experts on FLE agree that the responsibility for FLE rest with the parents of FLE into these programmes may achieve greater benefits of such efforts, which would directly have a bearing on the quality of our future generations.

Mani (1989), opined that NAEP curriculum should be a need based and participatory process. According to Wadia (1979) a need based NAEP curriculum sensitises the adolescent girls to their family conditions and will help them to widen their vision of themselves and to see their own individual and family circumstances in the light of the knowledge gained and act in accordance. Further, NAEP curriculum highlights home and family life as one of its content areas. A FLE curriculum based on perceived needs of experts of FPAI (1990) study revealed that majority of the parents do not accept the responsibility for providing FLE to their adolescent sons and daughters. Adams (1985) and Trivedi *et al.* (1976) stated that FLE should be taken up by the schools.

A review of Governmental and international agency programmes in India indicate that more emphasis is laid on health and nutritional status of adolescents. This could be because of their poor Health and nutrition status. The situation of rural adolescent girls in India possess major threat to the lives and growth of their children and themselves. According to NIPCCD (1990) for rural girls in India there is nothing as 'adolescences'. For rural girls end of childhood marks the beginning of adulthood. Adolescence has been regarded merely as a brief interlude between puberty and marriage. Gopalan (1990) advocated that public policy should focus on these young girls and on the health and nutritional status of women. He also stressed the need for 'education for better living and vocational training for rural adolescent girls'.

An examination of the literature presented in the section reveals that there are very few studies which focus on content, curriculum and methodology for development of FLE curriculum especially for Indian adolescent girls.

3

Methodology

Family Life Education (FLE) is a relatively new concept. It aims at promoting the quality of life through responsible decision making and improved understanding of human relationships and family roles. The term FLE has different meanings ranging from the narrow concept of education in family planning to the broader notion of education for leading a healthy, purposeful and constructive life. In a developing country like India, where conditions of poverty and ignorance are rampant and where the pressures and strains of life relate to mobilizing the basic resources necessary for mere existence, the concept of FLE assumes different ramifications. Exclusive programmes for promoting FLE are very few in India. However, FLE is taught as a part of certain educational programmes. There are, however, very few systematically developed curricula for FLE programmes. The curricula available, either emphasize population education, or population education and home science aspects. A need based curriculum would be highly relevant and meaningful to the learners.

Research Design

The present study is a participatory action research. It is a means of utilizing knowledge and research to institute changes and at the same time establishing an integrated relationship between theory and real life. Participatory action research helps to overcome many of the limitations of empirical research. Through participatory action undertaken at the community level, research becomes a process of empowering the target group and at the same time of generating knowledge. The essential factor in this approach to research is that it is a two way process. Awareness is created within the target group and utilizing their knowledge and awareness, the research programme is planned, documented and analyzed. Finally, the participants are provided a feed back so that they are empowered. The research design presented in Fig. 3.1, clearly outlines the research process of the present study.

Fig. 3.1
Family Life Education for Adolescent Girls Through the Non-formal Adult Education Programme (Chittoor Dist.)

Development of FLE Curriculum

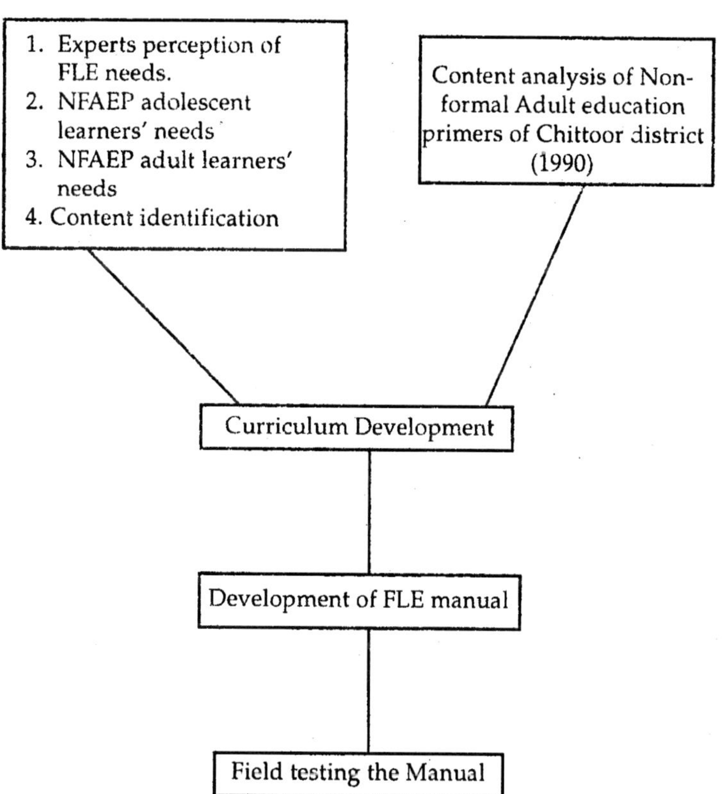

Locale of the Study

The Chittoor district in Andhra Pradesh was selected purposively for the following reasons.

- The researcher hails from the Chittoor district and, therefore, it is ideally suited to undertake participatory action research in the district;
- The Chittoor district is the representative backward district of the State in terms of the distribution of rural and urban population, degree of female literacy and other socio-economic parameters;
- Special adult education programmes were launched in the district under Total Literacy Campaign;
- Separate primers were exclusively prepared for this district and field tested.

The physiography of the Chittoor district is as follows: The district is bounded by the States of Karnataka and Tamil Nadu on all sides except on the northern and part of the eastern sides. It is one of the four drought prone districts of the Rayalaseema region of Andhra Pradesh. The district has an area of 15,152 square kilo metres and forms 5.5 per cent of the State area. Of this 14968.7 sq. km (98.79 per cent) is the rural area and 183.3 sq. km (1.21 per cent) is the urban area. The district is divided into 66 mandals covering 1485 villages. The population of the district is 32,56,247 (persons), of whom 80.18 per cent (26,10,987 persons) lived in rural areas and 19.82 per cent (6,45,260 persons) lived in urban areas. The female population is slightly less than 50 per cent of total population, i.e., 16,02,577 persons, of whom 80.3 per cent (12,83,923 persons) lived in rural areas and 19.7 per cent (3,15,651 persons) lived in urban areas as per 1991 census data.

According to the Chittoor Zilla Saksharata Samithi (1990) there were 49 per cent of male and 76.3 per cent of female illiterates out of whom 24.92 per cent of illiterates belonged to Scheduled Castes, 5.14 per cent to Scheduled Tribes and 69.94 per cent to other Castes. In spite of its meagre irrigation sources and relative economic backwardness, the district had witnessed a rise in female literacy rate from 37.6 (Census, 1981) to 51.8 (Census, 1991) which was well above the average all-state female literacy rate of 45.1 per cent (NIAE 1992). All the illiterates were made literate by August 1991, through the total literacy campaign launched on 2nd October, 1990.

Sample Selection

Multi-stage random sampling procedure was used for the selection of the sample from the 66 mandals of the Chittoor district which is shown in Figs. 3.2 and 3.3. In the first instance, 5 rural and 5 urban mandals were selected using tippets random sampling technique. From each mandal, 5 villages/areas were selected at random. From each village/area two married women aged between 20-30 years and eight unmarried adolescent girls, aged between 13 to 19 who were participants of NFAEP were selected.

The married adult women were chosen as reference group as it was felt that the adolescent girls might not perceive entirely their FLE needs clearly as they did not yet experience in the family life. Thus, the sample comprised of 500 NFAEP learners, out of whom 100 were married adult women and the remaining 400 were unmarried adolescent girls. A study of the married women vis-a-vis the adolescent girls was expected to generate the perceived FLE needs from two groups of women one with actual family life experience and another without actual family life experience, but ready to enter the family life.

Variables Selection

In this study, family life education needs are the dependent variables and the major independent variables are age, caste, type of family, family income, educational status, employment status, marital status and place of residence.

FLE Needs

The educational needs of the learners for Family life education as perceived by themselves and/or experts is called FLE needs. Perception of educational needs may vary depending upon the learners awareness, experience, exposure to the subject area and its relevance to their day to day life.

Age

Age is considered to be one of the proximate determinants of fertility. Davis (1964) felt that the socio-economic conditions of society are more important in influencing the age at marriage. Audinarayana (1985) found that literacy rate, employment status

Fig. 3.2
Sample Selection

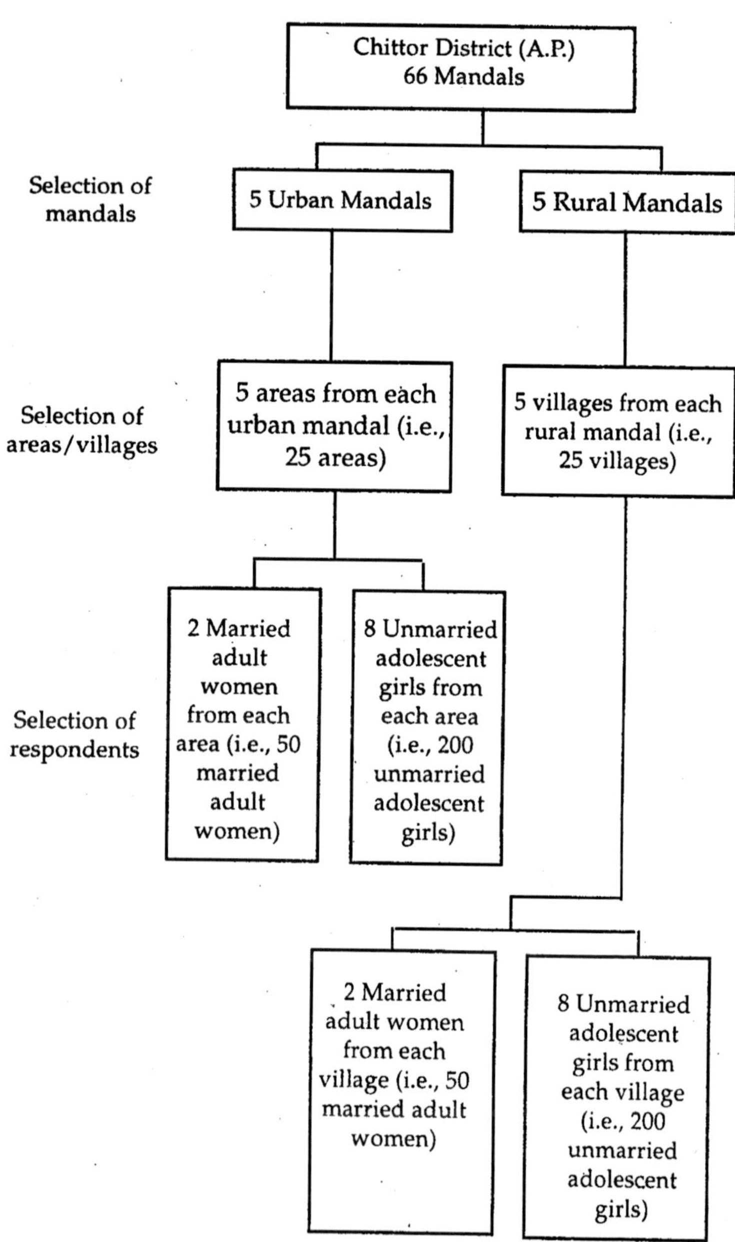

Fig. 3.3

Pie Chart for the Distribution of Sample Based on Marital Status and Locality

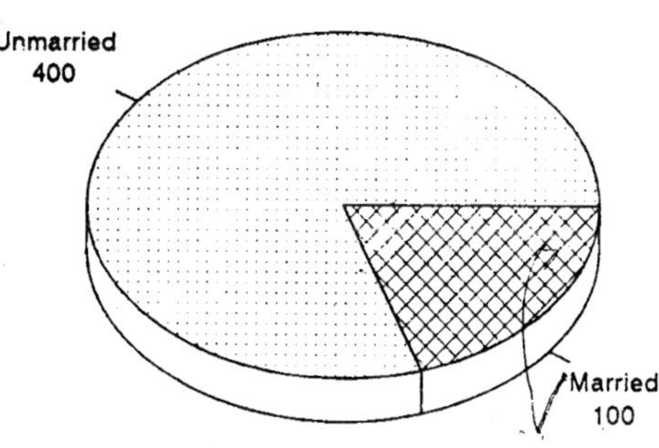

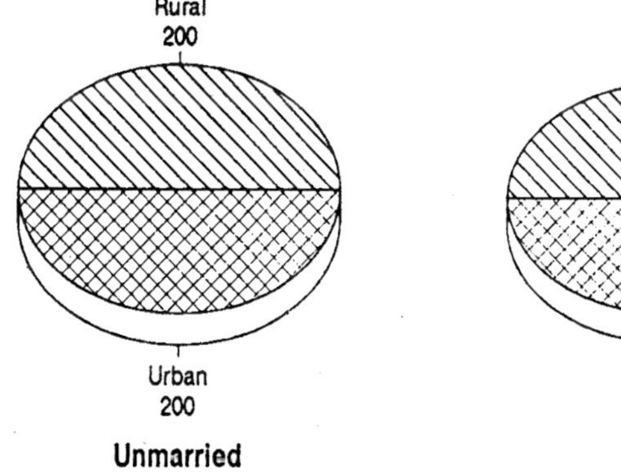

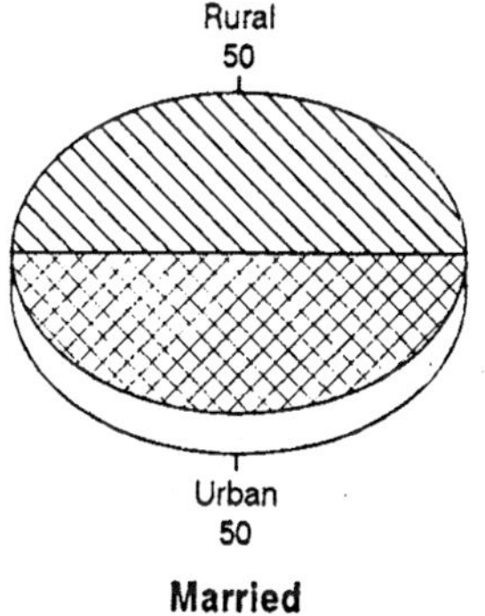

and the degree of non-agricultural employment as significant in influencing the mean age at marriage of males and females. This is understandable in view of the fact that a rise in the illiteracy rate reduces child labour in agriculture and increases school-going population. In addition, the growing literacy rate creates an awareness regarding family formation and fertility and leads to an increase in the age at marriage. Urbanisation also has a significant effect on female age at marriage. The income status of the women also influence the age at marriage. Therefore, following the earlier studies and on a prior reasoning age is included in the present study as an independent variable. Besides urbanisation promotes literacy, employment and income which in turn affect the age at marriage. It is well known that the process of urbanisation generates several changes in social values relating to the size of family, preference for children, attitude to work and employment which indirectly influence age at marriage.

Caste

Dahama (1976) defined "Caste as a collection of families or a group of families bearing a common name which usually denotes and is associated with a specific occupation, claiming common descent from a mythical ancestor, human or divine professing to follow the same calling and regarded by those who are competent to give an opinion as forming a single homogeneous community". Mazumdar (1962) has pointed out that in a country moored in traditions and dominated by stereotypes, where people are borne to castes and not free to form groups, where individualism has not asserted itself, institutional matrices and caste structure, cannot be ignored. Therefore, caste which influences most of the decisions relating to marriage is included in the study as a variable. For the present study, caste is classified into four groups, namely, scheduled castes, scheduled tribes, backward castes and others.

Scheduled castes group included the Malas, Madigas, Thotis, Mukchikes, Dakkalas (Madiga Priests), Dasari and Chalavadis (Mala Priests) and such other socially and economically backward groups subject to different kinds of discrimination.

The group of *scheduled tribes* include the detribalized castes, viz., Yerukalas, Yanadis, Lambadis, Batrajus Sugalis, etc., whereas, *backward castes* include artisan and service caste groups such as Kammaris, Kamsalis, Kancharis, Silpis and Vadrangis, whose work involves skilled labour were included. Service castes such as

Mangalis, Chakalis, Medaras, Vaddes, Boyas, Besthas, Idigas, Sagalis, Dommaras, Upparas and Satanis, engaged in service functions are included under this category. Finally *others* include Brahmans and allied caste groups, Kshtriyas and allied caste groups, Vaishyas and allied caste groups, caste Hindus or Sata-sudras.

Married and adolescent women were drawn from these four groups, in proportion to their relative representation in the total population.

Type of Family

Following the standard practice, in the present investigation, the families are classified into three types; nuclear, joint and extended. The term nuclear applies to family units consisting primarily of a husband, wife and their children. The families having related individuals of three generations, living in common residence, and where the males are related as father-son-grand children, are considered as joint family. The families consisting of a couple, their children and other dependents who are not co-sharers in the property or the family are considered as extended families.

The type of family, its size and composition are usually considered important in the analysis of demographic behaviour. Moreover, the type of family has a direct bearing on the awareness and exposure of the respondents. Hence, the type of family has an influence on perception of FLE needs of married and unmarried women.

Family Income

Nickell and Dorrey (1967) defined, "Family income as a stream of money, goods, services and satisfactions that come under the control of the family, to be used by them to satisfy their needs and desires and discharge obligations". Operationally, family income is generally measured in terms of annual income earned by the family members.

The size of family income indirectly influences the perception of FLE needs of women. An increase in income improves access of the adolescents to better education, mass media and social interaction. Hence, family income is included as a determinant of FLE need perception.

Marital Status

Entry or non-entry into the matrimonial state indicates marital status. Being married is a condition of man and woman legally united for purpose of living together and usually for procreating lawful offspring. While unmarried is a condition of girls/women not legally united and may not possess conjugal relationship. The matrimonial state influences the perception of FLE needs of unmarried and married respondents. A married woman is expected to possess greater awareness of FLE by virtue of her experience and exposure, whereas, an unmarried woman is generally not expected to possess knowledge, in any case, first hand knowledge of the family problems that go with the marriage. Therefore, marital status is included as an important parameter affecting FLE need perception.

Place of Residence

In urban areas, the family is generally aware of new ideas, attitudes and changes in life-styles. Urbanization gives the individual greater freedom of mobility and choice of employment and lessens the social pressures for conformity (Kelvin, 1971). Whereas, in rural areas, the kinship ties and traditions force the family to conform to village norms. The place of residence of the respondents has an impact on perception of FLE needs. Factors associated with urbanisation such as education, health and medical facilities, besides access to communication and mass media have a greater impact on the respondents in urban areas than in the rural areas. Therefore, the present study has included the place of residence as a determinant of FLE need perception.

Relationship Among the Independent and Dependent Variables

Very often, it is difficult to precisely determine the direction of influence of each variable. It is also common in socio-economic data that the variables cannot be grouped under well defined clusters or categories. Therefore an attempt is made to present the direct as well as indirect routes through which explanatory variables influence the dependent variables (Fig. 3.4).

Figure 3.4 shows that the age, caste, place of residence, type of family and family income influences the marital status. Place of residence and family income influences the respondent's exposure

Fig. 3.4
Relationship Among the Independent and Dependent Variables

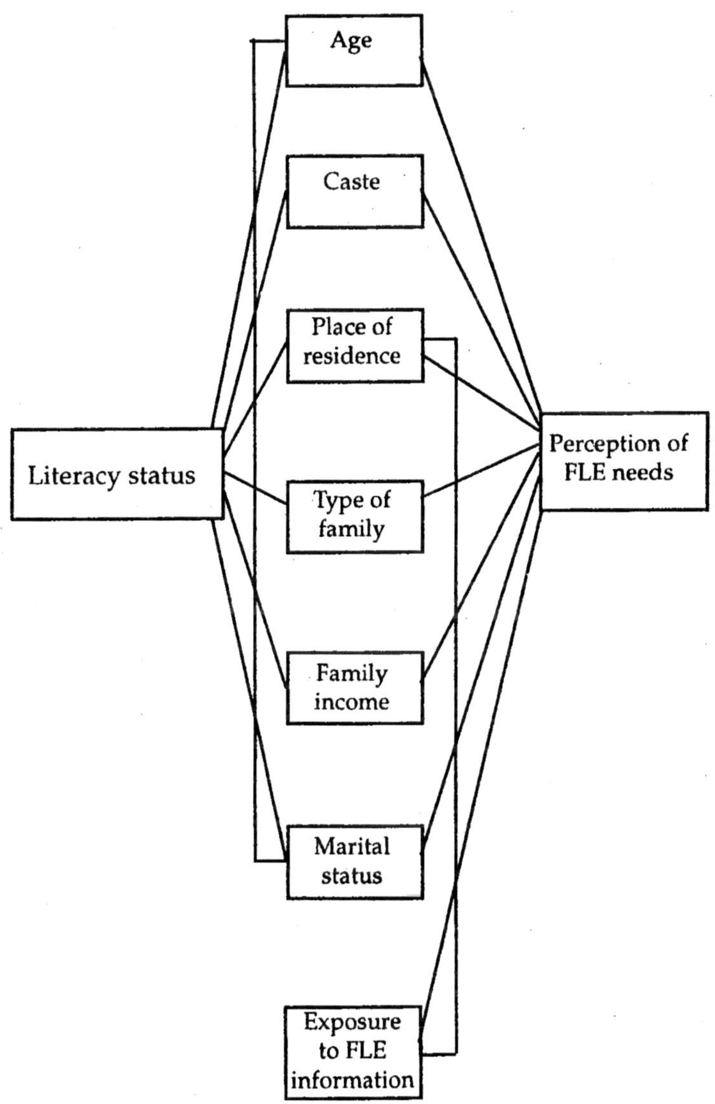

to FLE information. The exposure to FLE information influence along with other variables such as age, caste, place of residence, type of family and family income, perception of FLE needs. As the sample selected were neoliterates, educational status was not included as a variable in the present study. Yet, literacy status was shown in the figure, which was influenced by the independent variables such as age, caste, place of residence, type of family, family income and marital status.

Assessment of Variables

In order to assess the relative importance of FLE needs, an attempt has been made to construct an FLE need identification scale with the help of experts in the field of FLE. The FLE need identification scale was administered to twenty experts, conversant with the subject, for rating and prioritising the needs. The experts were drawn from the fields of home science, education, population education, social work, women's studies and adult education. The experts were asked to rate their perceptions on a three point scale.

The scale was translated into Telugu. A questionnaire was prepared to collect personal information about the respondents and their exposure to FLE information. The scale and the questionnaire were administered to a sample of 50 rural and 50 urban married adult women and 200 rural and 200 urban unmarried adolescent girls chosen at random. The subjects, both married and unmarried, were participants of ongoing non-formal adult education programme. The data relating to FLE needs of married women and unmarried girls were generated. The opinion or preference of each sample unit for the contents of FLE was ascertained and rankings assigned on the basis of mean scores obtained by each sub-sample on each topic. Thus, the mean score of strength of preferences, for each of the fifty topical areas was computed, of the experts, adolescent girls and married rural and urban women. The topics preferred most by the three groups were chosen for inclusion in FLE curriculum. The influence of independent variables, viz., age, family income, caste, type of family and marital status on perception of FLE needs was studied independently for married women and unmarried girls, with the help of Chi-square test.

Tools of the Study

The following tools were employed in the study :

FLE Needs Identification Scale (English and Telugu);
General Information Schedule;
Tool for FLE Content Analysis;
FLE Curriculum; and
FLEP Evaluation Schedules

FLE Needs Identification Scale

Experts in the field of family life education were interviewed to ascertain what in their opinion the content of FLE ought to be. Based on the expert opinion, 50 topics were identified, and grouped under 10 broad areas. A three point scale was chosen for the experts on the ground that a similar scale was employed for neo-literates. A neo-literate cannot be expected to possess the knowledge required to rate their preferences precisely on a finer scale. A three point scale was developed in English and was administered to twenty experts drawn from the fields of home science, population studies, women's studies, social work and adult education. The same scale was translated into Telugu, and field tested, revised. and then administered to 400 unmarried adolescent female learners (Comprising 200 rural and 200 urban girls) and 100 married adult women (Comprising 50 rural and 50 urban) learners of NFAEP.

Reliability of FLE Need Identification Scale

To compute the reliability coefficient of the FLE needs, identification scale, 'Test-Reset method' was used. Repetition of a test is the simplest method used to establish reliability of a scale. The scale was administered on a sample of 150 (comprising of 50 rural and 50 urban unmarried adolescent girls and 25 rural and 25 urban married adult women) and repeated on the same group after a month. The correlation computed between the first and the second set of scores and a reliability coefficient of 0.92 was obtained, which shows that there was highest correlation between the first and second tests.

General Information Schedule

A general information schedule was framed in Telugu together with personal information about the respondents and their exposure to FLE information. The schedule was also field tested, revised and administered on the same sample.

Tool for Content Analysis

The literacy primers that were developed for illiterate adults, are crucial for the success of NAEP. The importance of these materials lay in the fact that they were written for those men and women who constitute the poorest and most backward strata of society. In the case of IPCL primers that are now produced by State Resource Centres in the country, the content is presumed to have relevance for both men and women learners. Improved upon in July 1989, aimed at the integration of literacy, numeracy, functionality and awareness components in learning units with adequate scope for exercise, practice and tests, the IPCL material includes population education component which also forms part of FLE.

In the present study, the tool developed for content analysis of IPCL material by the National Institute of Adult Education (1991) was adopted to analyse the primers for FLE content. The IPCL materials developed exclusively for the Chittoor and Cuddapah districts in 1990 were used in the study. The IPCL material consisted of 3 primers, viz., Vachakamu 1, 2 and 3 and an instructional manual for volunteers/animators of NFAEP. Each primer had an introduction, author's note, index, lessons, illustrations, exercises, questionnaire and a certificate to be signed by the Mandal Co-ordinator (i.e., The Programme Co-ordinator at the Mandal level). The instructional manual of the volunteers/animators consisted of introduction by District Collector, author's note, a note on NAEP, called Aksharatapasman programme in Chittoor district. Initially, the primers collected were scanned keeping in view the objectives of the study. The lessons which have messages, pictures or illustrations related to FLE were identified. Finally, the component of FLE was analyzed with the help of the tool adopted and interpreted keeping in view the objectives of the study.

FLE Curriculum

Curriculum is a plan for providing sets of learning opportunities for persons to be educated. The term 'Curriculum' in its broadest sense refers to all the planned learning activities or experiences provided by an educational programme to a group of learners or target audience. As such it may include objectives, content, learning activities, materials, teaching aids and evaluating techniques and tools. A curriculum, in order to be relevant, must reflect the felt as well as the real needs of the target groups and also be within the framework of National goals for non-formal adult education programme.

Based on the findings of content analysis of NAEP primers (IPCL) and FLE needs of unmarried adolescent girl learners (as perceived by experts, married adult women and unmarried adolescent girls), a curriculum was drafted in the form of a manual to serve as a practical resource guide for animators/volunteers, who were intended to be involved in teaching/training/ communicating FLE. The animators manual (volunteerlaku suchanalu) of NAEP of Chittoor district was taken as a model for developing FLE curriculum, as the animators/volunteers were already oriented in the use of such manuals. Client oriented and expert oriented approaches were used in the development of FLE curriculum to ensure better participation of learners. Experts are most likely to be able to reflect the educational needs of the clients, because of their training and contact with clients, clients would be able to tell about their immediate needs and needs of their fellow citizens in the community.

The lessons that comprise the curriculum were derived from various manuals, handbooks, teacher guides and other forms of curriculum materials and reports that have been prepared in Malaysia, Philippines, India and some western countries, for use in their respective FLE programmes. Most of these lessons have been adopted to approximate their suitability to the Indian situation.

The curriculum divides 16 lessons into 7 units. The curriculum consisted of introduction, conceptual frame work, lessons, illustrations and evaluation schedules (See Appendix). The IPCL instructional manual for volunteers/animators was taken as a model for developing FLE manual for animators. The FLE curriculum (English) was translated into the local language (Telugu) and field tested on a sample of 30 unmarried adolescent girls, who were participants of NAEP. As the animator of NAEP has already trained in organisation of classes for the participants, has experience in the use of manuals and hails from the same area, she was chosen for conducting FLEP. The animator was oriented in the use of FLEP manual before launching the programme. The FLEP was conducted in Mangalam village of Tirupati rural mandalam for a period 3 months (i.e., from 1st May to 31st July, 1993) under the supervision of the Investigator. FLEP was conducted thrice a week (i.e., on Sundays, Tuesdays and Thursdays) for an hour. Thus FLEP needed 36 hours for completion. The impact of the programme is also assessed with the help of FLEP evaluation schedules.

FLEP Evaluation Schedule

To assess the FLE programme, a structured questionnaire consisting of 160 questions (i.e., 10 questions on each topic) was developed. The questionnaire was administered before and after the programme orally, as they were neo-literates. The initial and final knowledge scores of learners were recorded and computed.

Statistical Analysis of Data

Both qualitative and quantitative analysis of data was attempted. Qualitative analysis consisted of content analysis of NFAEP primers (IPCL). Further, Chi square test was used to study the association of independent variables with the perception of FLE needs. Mean and standard deviation and paired 't' test of initial/final knowledge scores of adolescent learners for each topic was computed.

Operational Definition of the Concepts Used in the Study Family Life Education (FLE)

FLE is an educational process designed to assist young people in their physical, social, emotional and moral development as they prepare for adulthood, marriage, parenthood, aging as well as their social relationships in the socio-cultural context of the family and society (IPPA, 1985).

Non-formal Adult Education Programme (NFAEP)

NFAEP is the process whereby persons who no longer (or did not) attend school on a regular and fulltime basis undertake sequential and organized activities with the conscious intention of bringing about changes in information, knowledge, understanding, skills, appreciation and attitudes, or for the purpose of identifying and solving personal or community problems (Liveright and May Good 1969). The NFAEP after attaining the status of a national programme is termed as National Adult Education Programme (NAEP). In the present study NFAEP and NAEP are used synonymously.

Animator/NFAEP Volunteers

Animator in a NFAEP is a person, who organizes the local NFAEP centre and works with the target population of learners.

Adolescent Girl

Females in the age group of 13 to 19 years were considered as adolescent girls. The adolescent girls who were not married were included in the present study.

Adult Married Women

Females who were married and have crossed the adolescent period, i.e., 20 years were considered as adult women.

Experts

Academicians conversant with the subject and possessing experience in conducting research in the area of FLE.

Curriculum

Curriculum is a set of planned learning experiences based on the nature of the learners to be educated, the society which provides and operates the educational programme and the accumulated knowledge available and feasible for educating learners.

Knowledge

Knowledge is a body of understood information possessed by an individual or by a culture. It is also that part of a person's information which is in accordance with established fact (English and English, 1958).

4

Results and Discussion

The study on "Family Life Education for Adolescent Girls through the Non-formal Adult Education Programme undertaken in Chittoor district during the years 1990 to 1993 has resulted in substantial data. The data has been analysed and discussed in the following.

Demographic Profile of Respondents

Age

The average age at marriage is a useful measure of the range of options to women such as, age at marriage, choice of mate, decision making in matters related to fertility, child rearing family planning and economic issues. A lower average age means fewer options; the woman is locked in early to the cycle of repeated child bearing. There is a clear relationship between a woman's age at marriage and her fertility (IUACE, 1990). According to Saxena (1989), age at marriage is inversely related to the length of child-bearing span and level of marital fertility. In this connection, one of the reasons accounting for higher level of fertility prevalent in India is its adherence to the pattern of early and universal marriage in respect of both boys and girls. Age also seem to influence the perception of FLE needs by girls/women. Hence age was included as one of the parameters in the present study.

On the basis of age, the sample of married adult women were divided into two age groups, viz., those falling under 21-25 years and 25-30 years. Similarly, on the basis of age, the sample of unmarried adolescent girls were divided into four groups, viz., those falling under 13-15 years, 16-18 years, 19-22 years and 23 years and above. The distribution of sample according to their age is presented in Fig. 4.1.

From Fig. 4.1, it is clear that nearly 90 per cent of the unmarried adolescent girls belonged to age group 13-15 and 16-18 years, while only a very small percentage of girls were above 19 years of age. This could be due to the lower age at marriage of girls. The mean age at marriage for females in the Chittoor District of Andhra Pradesh varied over the past four decades, viz., in 1961—16.34 years, in 1971—17, 14 years, in 1981, 17.98 years and in 1988—18.86 years (Goyal, 1988). This compares well with the data of the present study.

Caste

Following the standard socio-economic classification adopted by the government the married adult women and unmarried adolescent girls were divided into five groups, viz., scheduled castes, scheduled tribes, backward castes, economically backward castes and other castes. The other castes are in turn divided into economically backward castes and other. The distribution of respondents is presented in Fig. 4.2.

It is observed that among the rural unmarried adolescent respondents 30 per cent belonged to scheduled castes, 21 per cent to scheduled tribes, 14 per cent to backward castes, 14 per cent to economically backward groups and 21 per cent to other castes. Among the urban unmarried adolescent respondents, 29.5 per cent belonged to scheduled castes, 17 per cent to scheduled tribes, 19.5 per cent to backward castes, 17 per cent to economically backward castes and 17 per cent to other castes. This shows that comparatively good percentage of respondents belonged to scheduled castes. This pattern is not observed either among the rural or urban married adult respondents. Among rural married adult women 40 per cent belonged to other castes, 20 per cent to economically backward castes, 22 per cent to backward castes, 16 per cent to scheduled castes and only 2 per cent belonged to scheduled tribes. In contrast to this, among the urban married adult women,,30 per cent belonged to backward castes, 28 per cent belonged to scheduled tribes, 28 per cent to other castes, 10 per cent to economically backward castes and only 4 per cent to scheduled tribes.

Fig. 4.1
Distribution of the Sample Based on Age

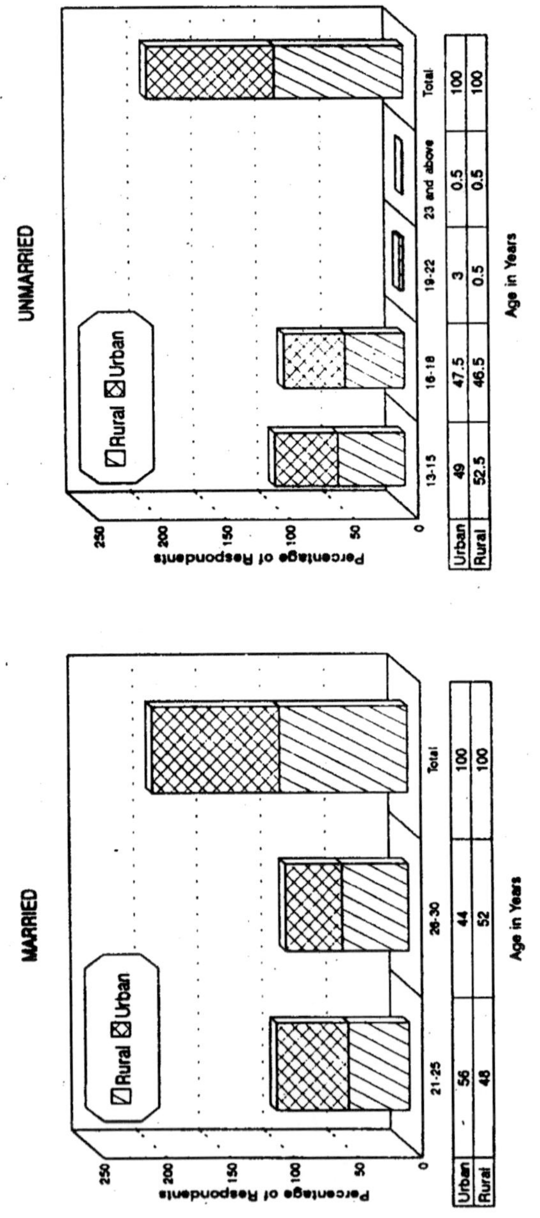

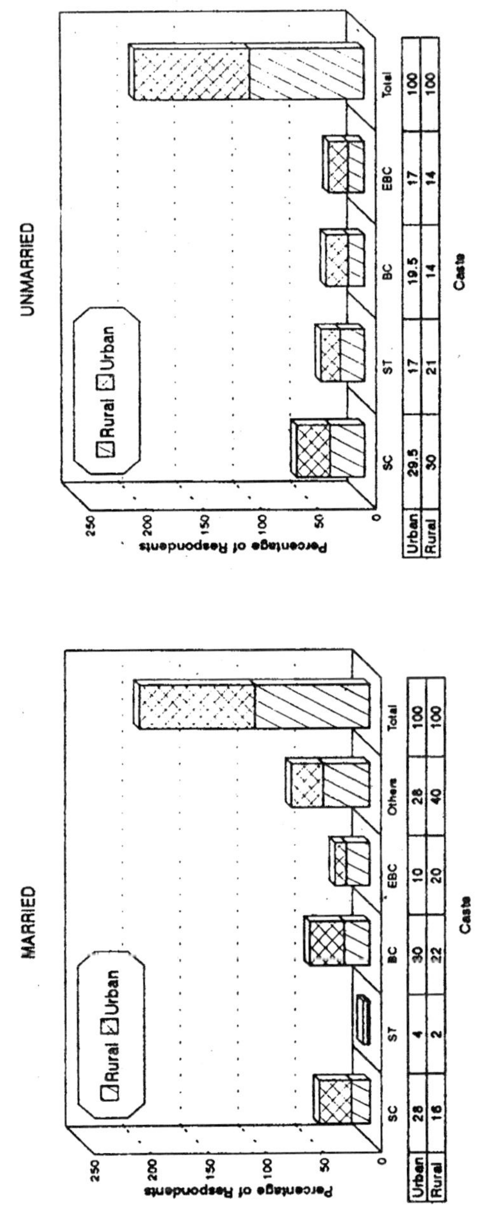

Fig. 4.2
Distribution of the Sample Based on Caste

Caste still remains in its pivotal position in the social structure of India, stratifying the society into a hierarchy of castes. It seem to influence the participation of girls and women in the NAEP. Hence caste was included as one of the variables in the present study.

Type of Family

Based on the type of family, the sample of married adult women and the unmarried adolescent girls was divided into three groups, viz., nuclear, extended and joint family. The distribution of sample by type of family (Fig. 4.3) shows that among the rural unmarried adolescent respondents, 72.5 per cent belonged to nuclear families, followed by 20 per cent to extended and 7.5 per cent to joint families. Similar pattern was observed among the urban unmarried adolescent respondents, where 60.5 per cent belonged to nuclear families, 38 per cent to extended and 1.5 per cent to joint families. The sample of married adult women also showed similar pattern. Among the rural married respondents 62 per cent belonged to nuclear, 36 per cent to extended and only 2 per cent to joint families. In the case of urban married respondents, 56 per cent belonged to nuclear families, 32 per cent belonged to extended and 12 per cent to joint families. The above distribution reveals that a major percentage of respondents belonged to nuclear families irrespective of their place of residence. This may be due to the structural changes that are taking place in the family system over a period. Findings of various researchers reveal that nuclear families are more among poorer households and landless castes (Kapadia, 1956, Sharma 1957, Mandelbaum, 1970 and Desai 1995). Literature on Indian family system always focused on joint family as a characteristic feature of the agrarian society. It is due to the change of occupations coupled with urbanisation, education, migration, etc., that joint family had given place to nuclear families. The type of family and the kind of environment that prevails in the family influences the perception of FLE needs of girls and women. Hence type of family was included as one of the parameters in the present study.

Size of Family

The family is composed of a complex of intractional systems made up of different members of the family, each of whom has a bearing

Fig. 4.3
Distribution of the Sample Based on Type of Family

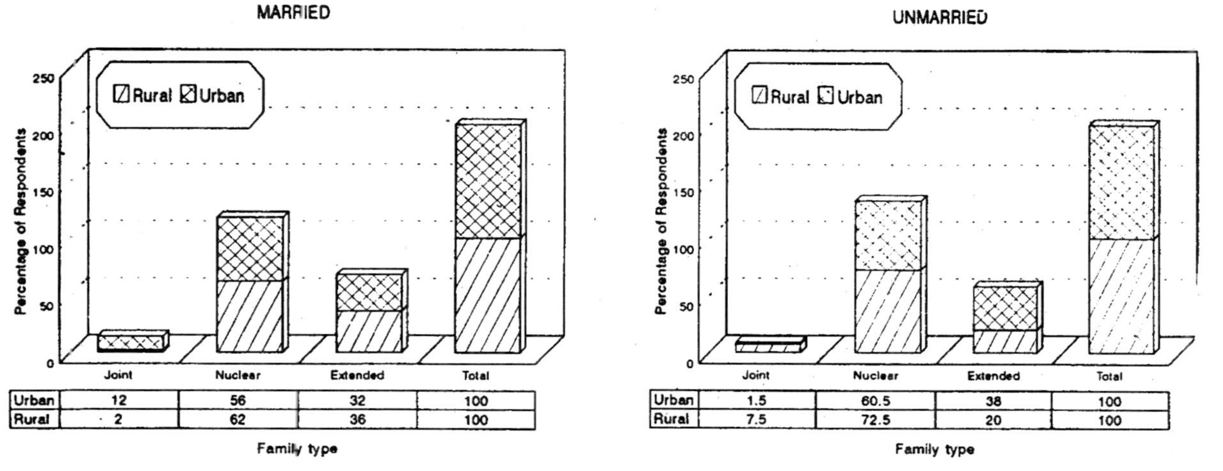

on the development of the personality and the behaviour of other members of the family. The larger the number, the larger is the interactional system. Each relationship and the interactional system has its own emotional quality which affects the members of the family involved in this system (Mahale, 1987).

The distribution of families by this size is presented in the Fig. 4.4, indicates that 66 per cent of rural unmarried girls, 80.5 per cent of urban unmarried girls, 28 per cent of rural married adult women and 36 per cent of urban married adult women belonged to the family size class of 5-10 members. Around 34 per cent of rural unmarried girls, 19.5 per cent of urban married girls, 72 per cent of rural married adult women and 62 per cent of urban married adult women belonged to families having less than five members.

The size distribution of families of unmarried adolescent respondents shows that a major percentage belonged to family size class of 5-10 members, which could be considered as large families. Contrary to this, a major percentage of married adult respondents had small families of less than five members. This difference in family sizes could be due to the fact that married women had more awareness and access to family planning methods, when compared to the parents of unmarried adolescent girls.

Demographic evidence suggests that the accurate determination of expected family size of a given population involves conceptual and methodological problems (McClelland, 1983). In most societies, few couples before becoming parents, plan the exact size of their families based on the costs and benefits of children and on their economic and personal resources (Ramu, 1988).

Family Income

On the basis of annual family Income, the married adult women/ unmarried adolescent girls were divided into five annual income groups measured in rupees, viz., less than 6,000, 6001 to 12,000, 12,001 to 18,000, 18,001 to 24,000 and 24,001 and above.

The economic status of a family frequently determines its social status. Figure 4.5 indicates that nearly 30 per cent of rural and 62 per cent of urban married women had a family income of less than Rs. 6000 per annum, i.e., lower than poverty line income level, 46 per cent of rural and 34 per cent of urban married adult

Fig. 4.4
Distribution of the Sample Based on Size of Family

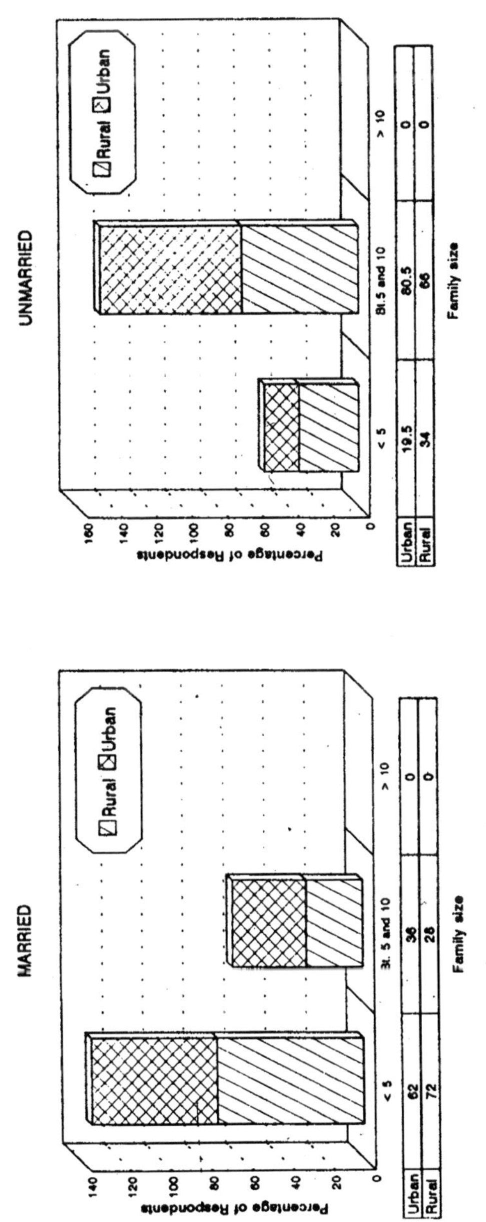

Fig. 4.5
Distribution of the Sample Based on Family Income

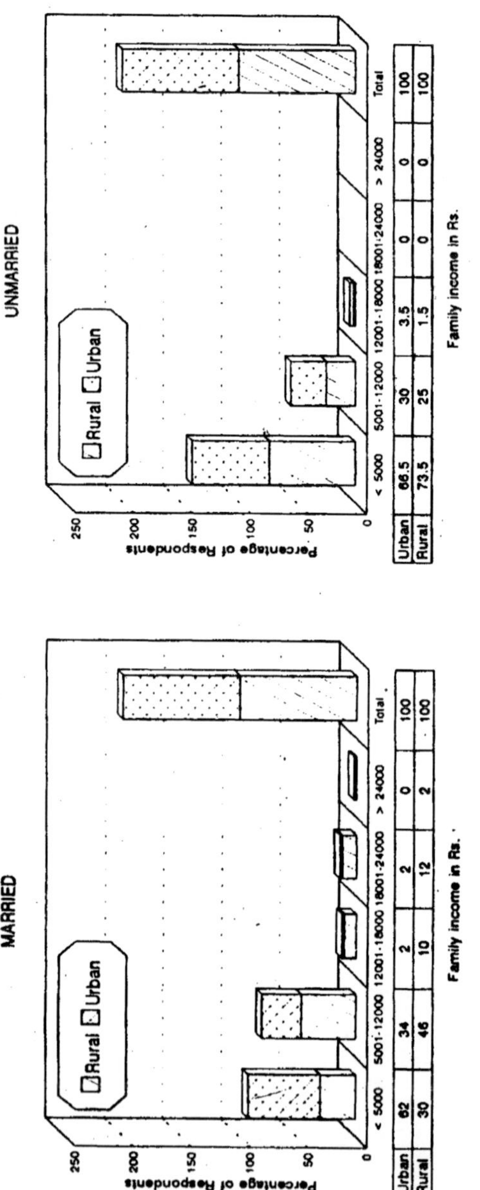

MARRIED

	< 5000	5001-12000	12001-18000	18001-24000	> 24000	Total
Urban	62	34	2	2	0	100
Rural	30	46	10	12	2	100

UNMARRIED

	< 5000	5001-12000	12001-18000	18001-24000	> 24000	Total
Urban	66.5	30	3.5	0	0	100
Rural	73.5	25	1.5	0	0	100

women had income levels ranging between Rs. 6001 and 12000. Only 10 per cent of rural and 2 per cent of urban married adult respondents had income levels between Rs. 12,001 and 18,000. The percentage of married women falling under the income levels of Rs 18001 and 24000 were 12 per cent in rural and 2 per cent in urban areas. A very small percentage of 2 per cent of rural married respondents had income levels above Rs. 24,001 and there were no urban respondents falling under this income level. The distribution of the data shows that the majority of married adult participants of NAEP belonged to low income groups, followed by middle income groups.

Similarly, in the case of unmarried adolescent girls, 73.5 per cent of rural and 66.5 per cent of urban respondents had family income less than Rs. 6,000. Around 25 per cent of rural and 30 per cent of urban unmarried girls had income levels ranging between Rs. 6001 and 12,000. Only 1.5 per cent of rural and 3.5 per cent of urban unmarried girls had income levels between Rs. 12,001 and 18,000. None of the unmarried girls had income levels above 18,000. Both the categories of the sample understudy had similar patterns of family income. This could be because, all the respondents were NAEP participants, who could not have the advantage of Formal Education due to several reasons, level of family income being to be one of them. For this same reason, family income was included as one of the parameters in the present study.

Respondents Exposure to FLE Information

Data on the respondents exposure to FLE information was gathered with the help of a General questionnaire which was administered along with FLE Identification Scale. The data generated has been analysed and discussed in the following.

Respondents' Opportunities to Know FLE Information

The response to the question "Have you had an opportunity to know about FLE Information ?" is summarised in Table 4.1.

From Table 4.1 it is evident that 86 per cent of rural and 74 per cent of urban married women did not have an opportunity to know about FLE information. Only 14 per cent of rural and 26 per cent of urban married women had opportunities to know about FLE information. Similarly, 79.5 per cent of rural and 73 per cent of urban unmarried adolescent girls did not have opportunities to know about FLE information. Only 20.5 per cent of rural and 27 per cent of urban unmarried adolescent girls had opportunities to know about FLE information. This data shows that there is a greater need for creating an awareness about and disseminating FLE information.

Table 4.1
Distribution of Married and Unmarried Respondents by Knowledge of FLE Information

Access to FLE information	*Married Women*		*Unmarried adolescent girls*	
	Rural	*Urban*	*Rural*	*Urban*
Yes	7 (14)	13 (26)	41 (20.5)	54 (27)
No	43 (86)	37 (74)	159 (79.5)	146 (73)
Total	50 (100)	50 (100)	200 (100)	200 (100)

Note : Figures in parentheses are percentages to total respondents

The respondents who had some information about FLE had largely gathered the same from mass media rather than through non-formal adult education.

Table 4.2
The Opportunities to Know FLE Information

Sl. No.	*Opportunities to know FLE information*	*Married women*		*Unmarried adolescent girls*	
		Rural	*Urban*	*Rural*	*Urban*
1	Adult Education Programmes	0 (0)	1 (7.7)	2 (3.9)	3 (5.6)
2.	Parents and Elders	1 (14.3)	1 (7.7)	5 (9.8)	2 (3.7)
3.	Friends	2 (28.6)	5 (38.4)	10 (19.6)	14 (25.9)
4.	Cinema/Radio/ T.V./Filmshows/ News papers	4 (57.1)	6 (46.2)	34 (66.7)	35 (64.8)
	Total	7 (100)	13 (100)	51 (100)	54 (100)

Note : Figures in parentheses are percentages to total respondents

The sources of FLE information are grouped under four heads, namely, Adult Education Programmes, parents and elders, friends and mass media (Cinema, Radio, T.V., Filmshows, News papers, etc.). Among the rural married adult women 57 per cent had known about FLE through mass media such as Cinema, Radio, T.V. Filmshows and News papers. 28.6 per cent through friends, 14.3 per cent though parents and elders and no one had indicated AEP as a source of FLE information. Similarly, 46.2 per cent of urban married women had opportunities to know about FLE through mass media, 38.4 per cent through friends, 7.7 per cent through parents and elders and 7.7 per cent through AEP.

Among the rural unmarried adolescent girls, 66.7 per cent had come to know about FLE through mass media, 19.6 per cent through friends, 9.9 per cent through parents and elders and 3.9 per cent through AEP on the other hand. 64.8 per cent of urban unmarried adolescent girls had opportunities to know about FLE through mass media, 25.9 per cent through friends, 3.7 per cent through parents and elders and 5.6 per cent through AEP. These responses indicate that mass media had been a predominant source of FLE followed by friends, parents and elders. AEP had a marginal role in fostering FLE.

Utilisation of FLE Information

The responses to another leading question "Have you utilised those opportunities?" are analysed and the result are presented in Table 4.3.

Table 4.3
Utilisation of FLE Information

Llitlisation of FLE information	*Married women*		*Unmarried adolescent girls*	
	Rural	*Urban*	*Rural*	*Urban*
Yes	2 (28.6)	4 (30.8)	1 (2.4)	2 (3.7)
No	5 (71.4)	9 (69.2)	40 (97.6)	52 (96.3)
Total	7 (100)	13 (100)	41 (100)	54 (100)

Note : Figures in parentheses are percentages to total responses

Table 4.3 reveals that 71.4 per cent of rural married women, 69.2 per cent of urban married women, 97.6 per cent of rural unmarried adolescent girls and 96.3 per cent of urban unmarried adolescent girls did not utilise the FLE information known to them. Only 28.6 per cent of rural and 30.8 per cent of urban married women and 2.4 per cent of rural and 3.7 per cent of urban unmarried adolescent girls had utilised the FLE information available to them. From the foregoing, it is evident that the percentage of respondents utilising the information had been very low and this could be either insufficient FLE information or lack of confidence on the part of women to practise the information. As the major source of information for the respondents was mass media, the respondents probably could not receive the entire information in a systematic way and had no scope to interact with the source and clarify doubts. This points to the need for imparting FLE through a communication approach where immediate feedback is possible.

Respondents' Special Efforts to Acquire and Practise

The information gathered about the number of respondents who have made special efforts to know and practise FLE information is presented in Table 4.4.

Table 4.4
Respondents Special Efforts to Knowing and Practising FLE Information

Special efforts to acquire and practise	*Married women*		*Unmarried adolescent girls*	
	Rural	*Urban*	*Rural*	*Urban*
Yes	3 (6)	4 (8)	12 (6)	27 (13.5)
No	47 (94)	46 (92)	188 (94)	173 (86.5)
Total	50 (100)	50 (100)	200 (100)	200 (100)

Note : Figures in parentheses are percentages to total responses

It is clear from Table 4.4 that 94 per cent of the rural and 92 per cent of the urban married women and 94 per cent of the rural and 86.5 per cent of the urban unmarried adolescent girls did not make any special effort to practise FLE information. Only 6 per cent of rural and 8 per cent of the urban married women and 6 per cent of rural and 13.5 per cent of the urban unmarried adolescent girls had made a special effort to know and practise FLE information. This could be due to lack of awareness about the importance of FLE information.

Sources Helpful to the Respondents in Their Special Effort to Acquire and Practise FLE Information

The ranks assigned by the respondents to the sources/persons who had helped them in their special effort to know and practise FLE information are presented in Table 4.5.

Table 4.5 indicates that among the rural married women, 66.7 per cent assigned first rank and 33.3 per cent assigned second rank to the mass media. While 33.3 per cent assigned first rank and 66.7 per cent assigned second rank to friends as sources of FLE information and help. Third rank was assigned to parents and elders by all the respondents. In contrast to this, only 25 per cent of urban married women assigned first rank and 75 per cent assigned second rank to mass media. 75 per cent of urban married women assigned first rank and 25 per cent assigned second rank to friends. All the urban married respondents assigned third rank to parents and elders.

The rural unmarried adolescent respondents assigned first rank to mass media, second rank to friends and third rank to parents and elders. Among the urban unmarried adolescents, all the respondents assigned rank one to mass media, 74.1 per cent assigned second rank to friends and 25.9 per cent assigned second rank to parents and elders. 25.9 per cent assigned third rank to friends and 74.1 per cent assigned third rank to parents and elders as sources of FLE information and help. Ranking trend reveals that the mass media was most helpful to the respondents in their special efforts to know and practise FLE information, followed by friends and parents and elders.

Respondents' Exposure to FLE through AEP

In response to the question "Were you taught FLE information in your AEP"?, 2 per cent of urban married women and 1 per cent of urban unmarried adolescent girls and none of the rural married

Table 4.5

Sources Helpful to the Respondents in their Special Effort to Acquire and Practise FLE Information

Sources helpful to Respondents in their special efforts	*Married women*						*Unmarried adolescent girls*					
	Rural ranks			*Urban ranks*			*Rural ranks*			*Urban ranks*		
	1	*2*	*3*	*1*	*2*	*3*	*1*	*2*	*3*	*1*	*2*	*3*
AEP	0	0	0	0	0	0	0	0	0	0	0	0
	(0)	(0)	(0)	(0)	(0)	(0)	(0)	(0)	(0)	(0)	(0)	(0)
Parents and Elders	0	0	3	0	0	4	0	0	12	0	7	20
	(0)	(0)	(100)	(0)	(0)	(100)	(0)	(0)	(100)	(0)	(25.9)	(74.3)
Friends	1	2	0	3	1	0	0	12	0	0	20	7
	(33.3)	(66.7)	(0)	(75)	(25)	(0)	(0)	(100)	(0)	(0)	(74)	(25.9)
Mass media	2	1	0	1	3	0	12	0	0	27	0	0
	(66.7)	(33.3)	((0)	(25)	(75)	(0)	(100)	(0)	(0)	(100)	(0)	(0)
Total	3	3	3	4	4	4	12	12	12	27	27	27
	(100)	(100)	(100)	(100)	(100)	(100)	(100)	(100)	(100)	(100)	(100)	(100)

Note : Figures in parentheses are percentages to total responses.

women and unmarried girls unambiguously stated that they were taught FLE information in AEP. This shows that the respondents who were exposed to FLE information through AEP belonged to urban areas.

Satisfaction of the Respondents with the Information Imparted in AEP

The respondents satisfaction regarding the information imparted in AEP was also gathered, which revealed that only 2 per cent of the urban married women expressed their satisfaction about the information imparted in AEP. None of the urban unmarried adolescent girls were satisfied with the FLE information taught in AEP.

Need for More FLE Information to be Taught in AEP

The responses to the question "Do you feel that more FLE information should be taught in AEP ?" are summarised in Table 4.6.

Table 4.6
Need for More FLE Information to be Taught in AEP

Need for more FLE information to be taught in AEP	*Married women*		*Unmarried adolescent girls*	
	Rural	*Urban*	*Rural*	*Urban*
Yes	26 (52)	33 (66)	167 (83.5)	152 (76)
No	24 (48)	17 (34)	33 (16.5)	48 (24)
Total	50 (100)	50 (100)	200 (100)	200 (100)

Note : Figures in parentheses are percentages to total responses

Table 4.6 shows that 52 per cent of rural and 66 per cent of urban married women and 83.5 per cent of rural and 76 per cent of urban unmarried adolescent girls felt that there was need for inclusion of more FLE information in AEP. Among the respondents who felt that there was no need to teach more FLE information in AEP were 48 per cent of rural married women, 34 per cent of urban married women, 16.5 per cent of rural and 24 per cent of urban unmarried adolescent girls.

From the foregoing, it is evident that majority of the respondents both married and unmarried had expressed the need for including more FLE information in AEP curriculum.

Need for Publication and Distribution of FLE Information in the Form of a Book

The data on the percentage of respondents feeling the need for publication and distribution of FLE information in the form of a book was gathered and presented in Table 4.7.

Table 4.7
Need for Publication and Distribution of FLE Information in Book Form

Need for Publication and Distribution of FLE information in the form of a Book	*Married women*		*Unmarried adolescent girls*	
	Rural	*Urban*	*Rural*	*Urban*
Yes	39 (78)	40 (80)	169 (84.5)	160 (80)
No	11 (22)	10 (20)	31 (15.5)	40 (20)
Total	50 (100)	50 (100)	200 (100)	200 (100)

Note : Figures in parentheses are percentages to total responses

Table 4.7 reveals that 78 per cent of rural and 80 per cent of urban married women and 84.5 per cent of rural and 80 per cent of urban unmarried adolescent girls expressed the need for publication and distribution of FLE information in the form of a book. Whereas, 22 per cent of rural and 20 per cent of urban married women and 15.5 per cent of rural and 20 per cent of urban unmarried adolescent girls did not feel the need for publication and distribution of FLE information in the form of a book. The majority of the respondents, however, felt the need for publication and distribution of FLE information in the form of a book.

Respondents' Exposure to FLE information Disseminated through Printed Media

The respondents' exposure to FLE information disseminated through print media was summarised as under. Of the total respondents, only 2 per cent of rural and 2 per cent of urban married women and 1.0 per cent of rural and 4 per cent of urban unmarried adolescent girls have seen illustrations related to FLE information and could read some information such as titles, captions and independent words in Telugu news papers/ magazines. As all the respondents were neo-literates, they may not have had the ability to read the whole information published.

Respondents' Exposure to FLE Information Broadcast through AIR (Regional Media)

All India Radio (AIR) is a government-run broadcasting set up taken up by the Indian Government in the year 1930. AIR comprises a countrywide net work of 205 centres and puts out 70 national news bulletins in 19 languages each day, 118 regional news bulletins in 22 languages and 33 tribal dialects and 63 bulletins in the external service in 7 Indian and 18 foreign languages—a total of 17,000 programme hours. Further AIR covers 79.8 per cent of the geographical area and 90.3 per cent of the population. Thus AIR has largest number of receivers than any other mass media in India (Kumar, 1994).

Almost all the respondents listen to the radio. The percentage of respondents who had the opportunity to listen to FLE information broadcast in Telugu (Regional Media) through All India Radio (AIR) was summarised and presented in Table 4.8.

Among the respondents, 6 per cent of rural and 10 per cent of urban married women and 16 per cent of rural and 17 per cent of urban unmarried adolescent girls had opportunities to listen to FLE information broadcast through AIR. The remaining 94 per cent of rural and 90 per cent of urban married women and 84 per cent rural and 83 per cent of urban unmarried adolescent girls have not heard any FLE related information on AIR programmes.

Respondents' Exposure to FLE Information Depicted in Telugu Cinema

Cinema is the main source of recreation of the majority of the people in Andhra Pradesh and also in India. The largest number of cinemas are produced in Telugu language. Commenting on this, Kumar (1994) stated that the reason for the big crop of films each year in Andhra is the State Government's support. It is perhaps the only state government that ploughs back about 7 per cent of the receipts from entertainment tax into film industry.

Table 4.8
Respondents' Exposure to FLE Information Broadcast through AIR (Regional Media)

Exposure to FLE information broadcast through AIR	*Married women*		*Unmarried adolescent girls*	
	Rural	*Urban*	*Rural*	*Urban*
Yes	3 (6)	5 (10)	32 (16)	34 (17)
No	47 (94)	45 (90)	168 (84)	166 (83)
Total	50 (100)	50 (100)	200 (100)	200 (100)

Note : Figures in parentheses are percentages to responses

Table 4.9 shows that the total respondents, 8 per cent of rural and 12 per cent of urban married women and 17 per cent of rural and 17.5 per cent of urban unmarried adolescent girls had opportunities to view FLE information depicted in Telugu cinema. The remaining 92 per cent of rural and 88 per cent of married women and 83 per cent of rural and 82.5 per cent of urban unmarried adolescent girls did not come across FLE information in Telugu cinema they have viewed.

Number of Cinemas in Which the Respondents have Viewed FLE Information

The responses to a question "In how many cinemas did you come across FLE related information in the last 12 months?" were summarised and presented in Table 4.10.

Table 4.9
Respondents' Opportunities to View FLE Information in Telugu Cinema

Opportunities to view FLE information in Telugu Cinema	*Married women*		*Unmarried adolescent girls*	
	Rural	*Urban*	*Rural*	*Urban*
Yes	4 (8)	6 (12)	34 (17)	35 (17.5)
No	46 (92)	44 (88)	166 (83)	165 (82.5)
Total	50 (100)	50 (100)	200 (100)	200 (100)

Note : Figures in parentheses are percentages to responses

Table 4.10
The Distribution of Respondents According to the Number of Cinemas in which they have seen FLE Information

Number of Cinemas	*Married women*		*Unmarried adolescent girls*	
	Rural	*Urban*	*Rural*	*Urban*
< 5	3 (75)	1 (16.7)	21 (61.8)	8 (22.4)
5-10	1 (25)	5 (83.5)	13 (38.3)	27 (77.8)
Total	4 (100)	6 (100)	34 (100)	35 (100)

Note : The Figures in parentheses are percentages to responses

From Table 4.10, it is evident that among the married adult women comparatively urban women viewed more number of cinema than the rural women. Similarly, among the unmarried adolescent respondents urban girls viewed more number of cinemas than the rural girls. This difference in viewing may be due to more accessibility to cinemas in urban areas.

A thematic classification of Indian films showed that 68 per cent of Indian feature films had social themes, which were obviously centred around familial problems (Mass Media in India, 1989-90).

Respondents' Exposure to FLE Information Disseminated through Filmshows

Data gathered on respondents exposure to FLE information disseminated through film shows revealed that only 2 per cent of rural and 6 per cent of urban married women have had opportunities to view filmshows related FLE. In the case of unmarried respondents, 5 per cent of rural and 14 per cent of adolescent girls also had opportunities to watch filmshows related to FLE. The number of filmshows viewed, for all the respondents was less than five. This indicates that the number of filmshows shown and the coverage of population was very small.

Respondents' Exposure to FLE Information Telecast in Doordarshan

In India, Television was started in 1959 on experimental basis to promote community development and formal education. In 1976, Television gained independent status under the new banner 'Doordarshan'. Now, there are 540 transmitters catering to 34.8 million T.V. Sets. According to the Ministry of Information and Broadcasting, the public television has "Dissemination of messages of family planning as a means of control and family welfare?" as one of the objectives. The objective is fulfilled mostly through Women and Health Programmes which occupy 1.9 per cent and 4.6 per cent of the total programmes of regional Doordarshan.

The data gathered on the respondents' exposure to FLE information telecasted in Doordarshan revealed that 8 per cent of rural and 12 per cent of urban married women and 38 per cent of rural and 40 per cent of urban unmarried adolescent girls had opportunities to view programmes having FLE related information.

The data on the frequency of respondent's exposure to FLE related programmes telecast was summarised, which is discussed as under: of the total respondents, 2 per cent of rural and 4 per cent of urban married women viewed less than five times in one year, while 3.0 per cent of rural and 7.5 per cent of urban married women viewed between 5 to 10 times. Only 2 per cent of rural and 2 per cent of urban married women viewed more than 10 times in one year. Whereas, in the case of unmarried adolescent girls, 19 per cent of rural and 5 per cent of urban adolescents viewed less than 5 times in one year. 15 per cent of rural and 27 per cent of urban adolescent girls viewed between 5 to 10 times in one year, and 4 per cent of rural and 8 per cent of urban unmarried adolescent girls viewed more than 10 times in one year.

Thus the data shows that the percentage of respondents and the frequency of exposure to FLE related programmes telecast through Doordarshan was very small. This could be due to inaccessibility to T.V. sets of a majority of households. Besides the inappropriate telecast schedule and urban and elite orientation of the T.V., programmes have alienated some of those respondents who had T.V. facility.

Identification of FLE Needs

FLE needs of unmarried adolescent girls identified by experts, married women and unmarried adolescent girls were ranked on the basis of mean scores obtained in each topic in each group. The topics which ranked high in all the three groups were chosen for inclusion in the curriculum as indicated below :

Concept of Family;
Functions;
Family Roles and Relationships;
Family Responsibilities;
Family Life Cycle;
Family Size;
Health and Nutritional Needs;
Psycho-social Needs of Family;
Management of Family Resources;
Menstruation and Changes in the Body;
Mate Selection;
Pregnancy and Child Birth;
Family Planning Methods;
Care of Children;
Good Parenting Practises; and
Family Welfare Services

The differences in perceptions of FLE needs by experts, married adult women and unmarried adolescent girls are discussed in the following.

Preferences of Experts, Married Adult Women and Unmarried Adolescent Girls for FLE Topics

Mean preferences of experts, married adult women and unmarried adolescent girls for FLE topics are presented in Table 4.11.

Table 4.11
Mean Scores Assigned by Experts, Married Adult Women and Unmarried Adolescent Girls for FLE topics

S. No.	Topic	Experts	Married Adult women	Unmarried adolescent girls
1.	Concept of Family	3.0	2.6	2.6
2.	Family Functions	3.0	2.6	2.6
3.	Family Roles and Relationships	3.0	2.6	2.4
4.	Family Responsibilities	3.0	2.7	2.2
5.	Family Life Cycle	3.0	2.5	2.5
6.	Family Size	3.0	2.6	2.4
7.	Health and Nutritional Needs	3.0	2.6	2.3
8.	Psycho-social Needs of Family	3.0	2.6	2.4
9.	Management of Family Resources	3.0	2.4	2.1
10.	Menstruation and Changes in the Body	3.0	2.7	2.2
11.	Mate Selection	3.0	2.3	2.3
12.	Pregnancy and Child Birth	3.0	2.0	2.2
13.	Family Planning Methods	2.7	1.9	2.1
14.	Care of Children	2.3	1.8	1.8
15.	Good Parenting Practices	1.8	2.4	2.4
16.	Family Welfare Services	1.7	2.3	2.3

The strength of preference of experts was relatively high for the first 12 topics (a mean score of 3.0), followed by topics 13 and 14 (mean scores 2.7 and 2.3 respectively). The experts assigned lowest ranks to topics 15 and 16 (mean score of 1.8 and 1.7 respectively). On the other hand, the married women exhibited highest preference to first 8 topics and 10th topic (mean scores ranged from 2.5 to 2.7), next preferred topics were 9, 15, 16, 11 and 12 (mean scores falling between 2.0 to 2.4) and lowest preference was given to topics 13 and 14 (mean scores 1.9 and 1.8 respectively).

The mean preferences exhibited by unmarried adolescent girls were high for the topics 1, 2 and 5 (mean scores ranged from 2.5 to 2.6). The next preferred topics wee 3, 6, 8, 15 (a mean score of 2.4), followed by topics 7, 11, 16, 4, 19, 12, 9 and 13 (mean scores ranged from 2.1 to 2.4) lowest preference was given to topic 14 (a mean score of 1.8).

From the foregoing, it is evident that the experts exhibited highest preference for the majority of the topics (14 topics), when compared with unmarried adolescent girls, the married adult women assigned high scores for majority of the topics. This could be because the experts and married women viewed the topics as more important than others due to exposure and experience. The data also reveals that there is variation in the preferences exhibited by the three groups.

Though differential FLE need perceptions were noticed among the three groups, the first 12 topics received top priority when compared to other topics by all the three groups. The differential perceptions of the three groups for each topic was discussed in detail as under.

Concept of Family

The family pattern in India is no longer predominantly joint. In recent years, certain important features of the family is ceasing to exist altogether in contemporary India. In urban communities, increasing employment of housewives and single-parent families have created a growing majority of families that have no adult at home throughout the day. Thus, many women are not available to perform their traditional activities including child care, care of other dependent social support activities and for unpaid work in the community. In this context, it becomes necessary to educate the new generation about the characteristics of present family to give the right concept about the contemporary Indian family. The mean scores for topic 1, namely, the concept of family shows that the experts exhibited highest preference (3.0), followed by married adult women (2.6) and unmarried adolescent girls (2.6). The experts due to their exposure to the findings of various studies on family could have felt, that understanding the concept of family as an important topic to be included in FLE curriculum.

Family Functions

Family functions are unique. The family may serve and has served in the past various functions. Its four functions are universal—sexual, economic, reproductive and educational. No society has developed a institutionalised pattern within which these functions are fulfilled by units other than the family. Training in family functions is necessary for every individual to discharge their functions as members of a family. This need is reflected in the preferences exhibited for the topic "Family Functions" by the three groups under study.

The mean scores of experts was 3.0, married adult women 2.6 and unmarried adolescent girls 2.6. Here again, the experts exhibited highest preference compared to married women and adolescent girls. Due to their exposure to wide range of studies in the area of family life, the experts might have realised the significance of family functions as one of the needed topics for inclusion in FLE curriculum.

Family Roles and Relationships

A role refers to an expected behaviour in any social interaction. A clear understanding of roles is very important in the family. Misinterpretation or lack of understanding leads to problems and sometimes crises. The issue of roles within the family is further complicated by changes in the family system, i.e., change from extended to nuclear/conjugal families, participation of women in economic activities outside the home, influences of western culture and religion, higher education, etc. Relationships are built overtime and is very dependent on role expectations. Family relationships can have devastating results on the development of children. Other than having negative effects on child behaviour, children also may have wrong impression of their respective roles as parents later on in their life. A well integrated programme on FLE can train the children to perceive their present and future roles correctly and develop a positive attitude towards their roles.

The mean preferences exhibited for topic 3, namely, family roles and relationships are as follows. The mean scores of experts is 3.0, married adult women 2.6 and unmarried adolescent girls 2.4. The unmarried adolescent girls showed comparatively lower preference. This may be due to their lack of awareness about the significance of the topic. On the contrary, the experts assigned highest score. This may be because the experts viewed family roles and relationships to be important for *a priori* reasons.

Family Responsibilities

Family responsibility for economic provision has important implications for the stability and quality of family life. It is important for the couples to coordinate the timing of marriage and career preparation and not to marry until they are able to support themselves. Family responsibilities and needs also influence the labour force participation of other members. According to Elder (1974) and Oppenheimer (1982), the extent and timing of women's labour force participation is still related to economic need and family composition. The economic activity of women in most cases tends to increase responsibilities both at home and work place. Thus, women are less available to perform their traditional activities, viz., child care, care of dependants, the provision of social support and the unpaid work in the community. Hence, there is a great need to train young girls and women to plan their work/career and family responsibilities in such a way that it does not affect the quality of their family lives.

For the topic of family responsibilities, the mean scores of experts was 3.0, whereas it was 2.7 for married women and 2.2 for unmarried adolescent girls. This suggests that the experts and married women viewed family responsibilities as more important as could be expected on *a priori* grounds.

Family Life Cycle

The Family Life Cycle or Family Career is a major concept in the family development frame work. The family career consists of several stages, each of which is characterised by specific developmental tasks to be accomplished. These tasks include physical maintenance, socialization motivation to perform roles, social control and addition and release of family members. Family career stages are mapped out in several ways according to family size and composition, marital status, ages and school placement of children and the employment status of major wage earners. Aldous (1978), Hill (1986) and Norton (1983) attempted to accommodate less traditional and non-nuclear family patterns into the family development frame work by incorporating divorce, remarriage, single parents and childlessness into the analysis of life cycle stages. Though the aforesaid stages are also prevalent in India, they are not desirable for a stable and quality family life FLE to youth to avoid such life stages in their family lives is very essential. This view is reflected in the scores assigned by the experts for this topic.

The mean preferences of experts, married women and unmarried adolescent girls for topic 5, namely, family life cycle was 3.0, 2.5 and 2.5 respectively. The scores show that experts accorded highest preference to family life cycle. The married women and unmarried adolescent girls due to lack of awareness may not have realised the importance of various stages of family life, which is seen in their ranking trend.

Family Size

The size of the family has been found to play an important role in the child's personality. Children from small families develop different personality patterns than those from large families. The larger the family groups, the greater the diversity of roles. In a large family, what role the child will assume will depend upon the roles already played by older siblings. The size of the family will also influence child rearing practices, emotional and economic security of the children, family integration and cohesiveness and parent-child relationships. Understanding the importance of family size the experts accorded highest score (3.0) to this topic for inclusion in FLE curriculum. Married women and unmarried adolescent girls assigned scores 2.6 and 2.4 respectively. The difference in mean scores of these two groups may be attributed to their marital status. The married women due to their experience may have realised the benefits of a small family and thereby assigned a better score than the unmarried girls. The mean preferences exhibited by the experts, married women and unmarried adolescent girls for topic 7, namely, health and nutritional needs was 3.0, 2.6 and 2.3 respectively. The experts assigned highest score, followed by married women and the unmarried girls assigned comparatively a lower score. This difference in preferences may be attributed to their levels of awareness of the role of nutrition in health.

Health and Nutritional Needs

Women are principal providers of care and support for infants and children in the Indian society as in almost every other society. Their role in child survival as agents of nutrition, protection, affection and development is crucial. The declining proportion of females to males in India is well known. According to the census of 1981 and 1991, the ratio of females to males was 934 females for every 1000 males and 929 females for every 1000 males respectively. In the matter of access to health and nutrition services, women get low priority. It is reported that for every three men who avail the health services, only one woman does so. Despite the percentages of sick women being higher than that of sick men at any given time, generally a woman is not seeking treatment unless severely ill. A survey in India by the National Committee on status of women found that women in 48.5 per cent of the households ate after men (Gopalan and Kaur, 1989). While summarising household surveys of individual diets in South Asia, Harris (1986) concluded that there is evidence on differentials on intrafamily food allocation and the explanation is essentially economic and cultural. To improve the health and nutritional status of women and young girls in India, there is every need to bring about changes in the patterns of food intake and utilisation of available Health and Nutritional Services.

The mean preferences exhibited by the experts, married women and unmarried adolescent girls for topic 7, namely, health and nutritional needs were 3.0, 2.6 and 2.3 respectively. The experts assigned highest score, followed by married women and the unmarried girls. assigned comparatively a lower score. This difference in preferences may be attributed to their levels of awareness of the role of nutrition in health.

Psycho-Social Needs of Family

The mean preferences exhibited for topic 8, namely, psycho-social needs of family by the experts, married women and unmarried girls were respectively 3.0, 2.6, and 2.4. Understanding the significance of psycho-social needs of family the experts accorded highest priority to the topic for inclusion in FLE curriculum. The married women who are presently experiencing the family life might have realised the psycó-social needs that could have been a reason for assigning a better score than unmarried girls, who due to the lack of experience may not have realised the importance of psycho-social needs.

Deprivation of psycho-social needs of family members, especially the children, leads to behavioural problems, viz., attention seeking behaviour, impairment of normal development of speech, intelligence and scholastic performance. According to Bowlby (1951), it is essential for mental health that the infant and young child should experience a warm, intimate and continuous relationship with his mother (or permanent mother substitute, one who steadily mothers him) in which both find satisfaction and enjoyment. Bowlby further emphasized that the actual physical separation from the mother in early childhood, to the extent that it involves privation or deprivation of a relationship of dependence with a mother-figure, will have an adverse effect on personality development, particularly with respect to the capacity for forming and maintaining satisfactory object relations. From the foregoing it may be suggested that as raising a family is a choice for today's women, only those willing to devote some years to this task should contemplate it, and they should then receive recognition for undertaking one of the most crucial tasks for society's future.

Management of Family Resources

The mean scores for the topic 9, namely, management of family resources were 3.0 for experts, 2.4 for married women and 2.1 for unmarried adolescent girls. These scores indicate that experts exhibited highest preference followed by married women and unmarried girls assigned comparatively a lower score. This must be due to lack of realisation of benefits of education about the topic on the part of unmarried girls.

Building house or house keeping, buying kitchen wares, vegetables or dress materials may require every detail of running the family. It is a decision as to what to buy and what not to buy. In most of the families, the husband passes on a monthly allowance to his wife and forgets about the family affairs until the next pay day is reached. With this allowance, the housewife has to meet the daily and monthly requirements of the entire family. While making her budget allocation, the housewife has to make a list of needs and priorities which are regular and also occasional. This situation calls for a proper orientation for women towards consumer philosophy. MacCracken (1989) pointed out that women seem to be particularly successful in better utilisation of natural resources, viz., water, fodder, fuel and in conservation of their environment rather than financial resources. This conforms well with the observations of Rodd (1988), who stated that, many women in developing countries have direct contact with natural environment as they collect essential items, viz., fuel, food and fodder for their every day needs. If these women are educated on sound lines they will manage the natural resources around them judiciously. These observations of researchers tallied with the scores assigned by experts for the topic for inclusion in FLE curriculum.

Menstruation and Changes in the Body

The two outstanding aspects of adolescence and youth are the capacity for reproduction and of full physical participation in work. The age of onset of menstruation was studied by several researchers. Robert (1977) made a study on menarcheal age in Southern India and found that the difference in median age in most schools was 12-16 years. Vidya's (1980) study on the factors influencing the age of menarche, revealed that there is a close relationship between family income and menarcheal age. The better health and nutritional status of the girls in these families is one of the reasons for lower menarcheal age. A good percentage of adolescent girls suffer from premenstrual syndrome which is a functional symptom complex consisting of cyclic irritability, depression and lethargy. According to Mathai (1992), if girls during menstruation do not observe cleanliness, their womb may get illnesses which may lead to childlessness. They can even get illnesses like tetanus and die. These findings stress the need for educating the young girls to adopt healthy behavioural styles to lead a healthy life.

The mean preferences of experts, married women and unmarried adolescent girls for the topic 10, namely, menstruation and changes in the body were 3.0, 2.7 and 2.2 respectively. From these scores, it is evident that the adolescent girls who would have entered this stage recently exhibited comparatively lowest preference. Married women, who would have adjusted to this stage by now exhibited greater preference than adolescent girls. The experts assigned highest scores than the other two groups. This may be attributed to their exposure and experiences for *a priori* reasons.

Mate Selection

The mean preferences exhibited by experts, married women and unmarried adolescent girls for the topic 11, namely, mate selection is 3.0, 2.3 and 2.3, respectively. The experts exhibited comparatively highest preference for the topic. The mean scores of married women and unmarried girls for the topic was almost the same. The reason for the comparatively lowest preference of the topic, by the married women and unmarried girls could be the continuation or practice of arranged marriages in the society. This compares well with the studies of Ross (1961) and Parmar (1987) which states that marriage is regarded as the most important social institution among the Indians not because it regulates sexual life but it helps in fulfilment of religious and social duties. Marriage contract was looked upon as an agreement between two families rather than between two young people (Ross, 1961). It was the responsibility of the family and not the party concerned to arrange the marriages of boys and girls as soon as they attained the marriageable age and hence the matter was considered at the family level. Thus, it is obvious that the selection of mates for the marriage was a family matter and there was not much provision for individual choice. This trend in selection of mate was observed by Ramu (1988) in Indian families residing in urban areas, having high educational and occupational accomplishments and exposure to western ways. The Indian communities, despite their residence in Britain seemed to maintain ethnic identity in marriage issues. Goldthorpe (1987) viewed arranged marriage as a crucial issue born within South Asian Communities and between them and the host society (Britain).

Pregnancy and Child Birth

The desire to bear and rear children was universal among the couples who sincerely believed that they had a moral obligation to procreate. Moreover children were perceived as a cementing force between spouses and an expression of conjugal love and an important part of marital interaction. Pregnancy and child birth are two stressful stages in a woman's life. Women require preparation for these stages, well before they enter marital life. In the present study, this need was more felt by the experts than the other two groups. The mean scores of experts was 3.0, married women 2.0 and unmarried adolescent girls 2.2. These scores indicate that the experts exhibited highest preference followed by unmarried girls and the married women exhibited comparatively lowest preference. The experts exposure to vast information about this stage of life (pregnancy and child birth) highlighting its impact on the future of the child born, could be the reason for according highest preference. Married women, who are women, who are presently experiencing these stages, due to lack of exposure, may not have realised the implications of this stage and that would have been the reason for exhibiting comparatively lower preference for the topic.

Family Planning Methods

The successful limitation of family size by the couples depends not only on their small family norms but also on their psychological acceptance of family limitation, knowledge of birth control methods, availability of contraceptives, psychological and economic costs and more importantly an environment favourable to the practice of birth control.

For the topic 13 on family planning methods, the mean preferences exhibited by experts was 2.7, married women 1.9 and unmarried adolescent girls 2.1. The mean scores indicate that the experts exhibited highest preference, followed by unmarried girls and married women exhibited lowest preference. This conforms well with the studies of Pareek and Rao (1974), Mandelbaum (1974), Jain (1975), Mitra (1978) and Mahadevan (1979) which indicated that the vast majority of Indians are aware of at least one method of birth control. This could be the reason for low mean scores of married women. The unmarried girls due to lack of experience and curious to know about family planning methods might have assigned a better score than married women.

Care of Children

Low maternal education, poor housing, unsatisfactory environmental sanitation, poor personal hygiene, poverty, ignorance makes the children fall prey to diseases like respiratory infections, gastro intestinal disorders, skin diseases, worm infestations and malnutrition. The health and nutritional status of a person mostly depends on his/her health status in childhood. Hence, it is necessary, to educate the young girls on these lines who are on the threshold of marriage and motherhood.

For the topic 14, namely, care of children the mean preferences of experts, married women and unmarried adolescent girls were 2.3, 1.8 and 1.8 respectively. The married women and unmarried adolescent girls exhibited lower preference for the topic than the experts. This difference in perceptions could be attributed to the awareness and exposure to the information related to care of children.

Good Parenting Practices

The familial environment especially the prevailing parental attitude or emotional tone of parent child interactions, has long been identified as an important factor in understanding child development. It is related to a variety of child variables such as independence, self-esteem, moral development, anxiety, conduct problems and school adaptation and achievement. In India due to the indulgent behaviour of the mothers, most Indian children do not have the gradual, step by step experiences, of many small frustrations and disappointments, which form a normal part of the life experiences of children in the western countries.

The mean preferences exhibited for the topic 15, on good parenting practices by experts was 1.8, married adult women 2.4 and unmarried adolescent girls 2.4. The pattern of preference indicates that unlike the earlier topics, this was given comparatively higher preference by married and unmarried respondents.

Family Welfare Services

In India, family welfare services are mainly rendered through government programmes. Based on the national problems and policies, these family welfare programmes are planned and implemented through Government and Non-Government organisations. The prominent among the Family Welfare Services are Immunization, pre and post natal care, Family Planning and family guidance and counselling services. Despite of wide publicity the utilisation of these services by women are poor. This may be due to lack of awareness and diffidence on the part of women. This situation calls for a well integrated education programme on family welfare services.

The preferences of experts, married women and unmarried adolescent girls for the topic 16, namely, Family Welfare Services was 1.7, 2.3 and 2.3 respectively, unlike the other topics the married and unmarried girls exhibited highest preference than the experts. This scoring pattern compares well with the above discussion. The need for inclusion of this topic in FLE curriculum is more felt by the learners than the experts. This may be because the experts expected the participants to realise their needs and avail the services extended by the government to fulfil those needs.

Impact of Socio-economic Background of Married Women and Unmarried Adolescent Girls on FLE Need Perceptions

The association of independent variables, viz., age, caste, type of family, family income and marital status with perception of FLE needs was examined independently for married women and unmarried adolescent girls with the help of Chi-square test. The results are presented in the following sub-sections.

Age and FLE Need Perception

Table 4.12, shows that there is no significant difference in the perceived FLE needs of married women of two age groups, except for topic, "Pregnancy and Child birth", for which statistically significant difference was observed between the perceptions of two groups. This indicates that age was not significantly associated with their perception of FLE needs of married women.

Table 4.12
Association of Age with Perception of FLE Needs of Married Women and Unmarried Adolescent Girls : χ^2 Values

S. No.	*FLE Topics*	*χ^2 Value*	
		Married women	*Unmarried adolescent girls*
1.	Concept of Family	1.1750@	6.2960*
2.	Family Functions	0.0369@	0.6866@
3.	Family Roles and Relationships	0.2123@	3.9080@
4.	Family Responsibilities	0.6242@	4.4200@
5.	Family Life Cycle	0.5307@	3.6600@
6.	Family Size	0.7301@	0.8159@
7.	Health and Nutritional Needs of Family	2.7070@	0.2237@
8.	Psycho-social Needs of Family	0.4548@	0.2842@
9.	Management of Family Resources	0.4589@	6.5478@
10.	Menstruation and Changes in the Body	0.8132@	4.4250@
11.	Mate Selection	2.3310@	0.9157@
12.	Pregnancy and Child Birth	6.0470*	1.8940@
13.	Family Planning	1.6070@	2.3390@
14.	Care of Children	3.8790@	13.6600**
15.	Good Parenting Practices	0.0983@	2.6890@
16.	Family Welfare Services	0.1925@	0.6997@

Notes : @Not significant; *Significant at 0.05 level; **Significant at 0.01 level

There is no significant difference between the two age groups of unmarried girls in their perception of FLE needs for 13 topics. Significant difference was found for topics "Concept of Family" and "Management of Family Resources" at 0.05 level and for the topic "Care of Children" at 0.01 level. These indicate that significant association was found for age with their perception for only three FLE topics.

This difference in perception between married women and unmarried girls may be attributed to their marital status.

Family Income and FLE Need Perception

On the basis of family income, the sample of married women/ unmarried girls was divided into five groups, viz., less than Rs. 6,000 and Rs. 6,001 to 12,000, Rs. 12,001 to 18,000, Rs. 18,001 to 24,000 and Rs. 24,000 and above per annum. The Chi-square values for the married women category for all the 16 topics (Table 4.13) shows that there is no significant difference between the level of income and perception of FLE needs.

In the case of unmarried girls, significant difference was observed between the income groups for 7 topics at 0.01 level and for 4 topics at 0.05 level. No significant difference was found between the income groups for 5 topics. This indicates that the family income influences the perception of FLE needs of unmarried girls. Similar influences were not found to exist in married women. This may be attributed to respondents' marital status.

Caste and FLE Need Perception

On the basis of caste, the sample of married women and unmarried girls was divided into five groups. As the size of the sample falling under each category was too small to apply the statistical tests, they were grouped into three categories, viz., scheduled castes/ scheduled tribes, backward castes/economically backward classes and others.

From Table 4.14, it can be observed that the caste is significantly associated with their perception of FLE needs for inclusion in FLE curriculum. In the case of unmarried adolescent girls significant difference can be observed between caste and perception of FLE need for topics, 1, 11 and 13. No significant difference is noticed for the remaining 13 topics. This may be due to their marital status, i.e., unmarried. Dhar (1982), also indicated low percentage of knowledge content among non-school going adolescent girls, in all areas of population and family life related issues.

Type of Family and FLE Need Perception

Based on the type of family, the entire sample of married women/

Table 4.13
Association of Family Income with Perception of FLE Needs of Married Women and Unmarried Adolescent Girls : χ^2 values

S. No.	*FLE Topic*	*χ^2 Value*	
		Married women	*Unmarried adolescent girls*
1.	Concept of Family	0.1845@	1.1660@
2.	Family Functions	0.05044@	0.04347@
3.	Family Roles and Relationships	0.3850@	0.7868@
4.	Family Responsibilities	0.01842@	19.4500@
5.	Family Life Cycle	0.8248@	7.8170*
6.	Family Size	0.2536@	8.0260*
7.	Health and Nutritional Needs of Family	1.3860@	114.700**
8.	Psycho-social Needs of Family	3.2150@	6.8380*
9.	Management of Family Resources	0.8430@	3.4430@
10.	Menstruation and Changes in the Body	0.3380@	40.2000**
11.	Mate Selection	1.1580@	17.8100**
12.	Pregnancy and Child Birth	2.2120@	20.6900**
13.	Family Planning	1.2100@	12.9300**
14.	Care of Children	2.9050@	3.7450**
15.	Good Parenting Practices	0.0983@	2.689@
16.	Family Welfare Services	5.1450@	7.4710*

Notes :@Not significant
*Significant at 0.05 level.
**Significant at 0.01 level.

unmarried girls was divided into two groups, viz., joint/extended family and nuclear family. The association between types of family and FLE needs observed is presented in Table 4.15.

It can be observed that there is no significant difference between type of family and perception of FLE needs among married women. In the case of unmarried girls, significant difference was found for only two topics at 0.01 level. No significant difference was found for remaining 14 topics, which may also be attributed to their marital status, i.e., unmarried.

Marital Status and FLE Need Perception

The association between marital status and perception of FLE

Curriculum needs was sought and assessed by using Chi-square test for a sample of 400 unmarried adolescent girls and 100 married women and their perceived needs and the results are presented in the following.

Table 4.14
Association of Caste with Perception of FLE Needs of Married Women and Unmarried Adolescent Girls : χ^2 values

S. No.	FLE Topics	χ^2 Value	
		Married women	Unmarried adolescent girls
1.	Concept of Family	1.3340@	14.1500**
2.	Family Functions	1.64204@	5.3080@
3.	Family Roles and Relationships	0.9081@	1.1720@
4.	Family Responsibilities	1.2410@	4.9950@
5.	Family Life Cycle	1.4300@	6.9100@
6.	Family Size	2.5830@	5.5160@
7.	Health and Nutritional Needs of Family	0.4579@	4.6780@
8.	Psycho-social Needs of Family	1.0670@	5.1640@
9.	Management of Family Resources	1.5840@	2.7600@
10.	Menstruation and Changes in the Body	2.0590@	2.1030@
11.	Mate Selection	0.8800@	31.3000**
12.	Pregnancy and Child Birth	2.9010@	8.9050@
13.	Family Planning	5.7510@	15.1700**
14.	Care of Children	4.1660@	8.5880@
15.	Good Parenting Practices	2.1330@	5.7250@
16.	Family Welfare Services	6.4720@	4.8220@

Notes : @Not significant
*Significant at 0.05 level.
**Significant at 0.01 level.

Table 4.16, reveals that the perceived FLE needs for inclusion in the FLE curriculum by married women/unmarried girls was significantly associated with their marital status. Thus, only with regard to first two topics the null hypothesis was not accepted and for all the 12 topics it was accepted.

Content Analysis of NAEP Primers of Chittoor District (Andhra Pradesh)

The content analysis of NAEP primers is one of the important

Table 4.15
Association of Type of Family with Perception of FLE Needs of Married Women and Unmarried Adolescent Girls : χ^2 values

S. No.	*FLE Topics*	*χ^2 Value*	
		Married women	*Unmarried adolescent girls*
1.	Concept of Family	0.8279@	3.6300**
2.	Family Functions	1.4060@	4.6070@
3.	Family Roles and Relationships	0.5305@	2.5750@
4.	Family Responsibilities	0.1917@	0.3020@
5.	Family Life Cycle	2.9920@	13.5800@
6.	Family Size	0.5884@	3.0920@
7.	Health and Nutritional Needs of Family	0.4597@	4.4590@
8.	Psycho-social Needs of Family	3.2070@	2.8120@
9.	Management of Family Resources	1.7760@	3.6400@
10.	Menstruation and Changes in the Body	1.1260@	0.7740@
11.	Mate Selection	1.7820@	1.5150@
12.	Pregnancy and Child Birth	0.6536@	0.02341@
13.	Family Planning	1.6730@	1.5140@
14.	Care of Children	1.8510@	1.6020@
15.	Good Parenting Practices	4.3550@	2.7680@
16.	Family Welfare Services	0.0928@	9.7110**

Notes : @Not significant
*Significant at 0.05 level.
**Significant at 0.01 level.

aspects of the study. As explained earlier, the study deals in Chittoor district. The NAEP teaching material consisted of three primers (Texts 1, 2, and 3) and a guidance manual (Instructions to Volunteers) for animators/volunteers. The teaching material is written and taught in Telugu language.

On the basis of the sixteen topics identified and by using the "tool of content, analysis, the three primers and the guidance manual of NAEP of Chittoor District (1990) were subject to critical analysis. NAEP primers are intended to include and integrate population education component of which FLE is also a part. Population education as part of NAEP primers is intended to bring about desirable changes in knowledge, understanding, attitudes and practices of learners relating to population matters. It was

Table 4.16
Association of Type of Marital Status with Perception of FLE Needs of Married Women and Unmarried Adolescent Girls : χ^2 values

S. No.	*FLE Topics*	*χ^2 Value*
1.	Concept of Family	3.4370@
2.	Family Functions	4.781@
3.	Family Roles and Relationships	26.960**
4.	Family Responsibilities	65.1500**
5.	Family Life Cycle	10.0800**
6.	Family Size	19.7000**
7.	Health and Nutritional Needs of Family	36.0200**
8.	Psycho-social Needs of Family	33.9700**
9.	Management of Family Resources	52.0200**
10.	Menstruation and Changes in the Body	59.0200**
11.	Mate Selection	8.6410*
12.	Pregnancy and Child Birth	41.7000**
13.	Family Planning	17.0800**
14.	Care of Children	23.7900**
15.	Good Parenting Practices	6.9370*
16.	Family Welfare Services	12.5400**

Notes : @Not significant
*Significant at 0.05 level.
**Significant at 0.01 level.

with this in view that the content of FLE was analysed in the study. More specifically the objectives of content analysis were :

- to identify the FLE content if any, in NAEP primers;
- to analyse or categorize or classify the content into different areas or sub-areas of FLE; and
- to suggest topics or issues or messages, etc., on FLE for adequate coverage or inclusion or integration in IPCL primers.

The tool for content analysis on NAEP primers for FLE content consisted for ten questions. The answers to these questions were identified by examining the NAEP. primers, which were presented and discussed as under:

- a very small portion of FLE content was integrated in the NAEP primers;

- it was integrated in two of the primers (1 and 3);
- FLE content was introduced in topic 8, "What happens when Population Increases" (*Janam Perigithe Emavuthundo Thelusa*) of primer 1 and topic 7, "To be healthy" (*Arogyamga vundalante*) of primer 3. In topics 8 of primer 1, FLE content was introduced in the form of independent words, sentences, non-verbal messages (through illustrations) and slogans. Whereas, in topic 7 of primer 3, FLE content was introduced in the form of a story and also independent words, sentences and non-verbal messages. In both the topics 7 and 8, the content was integrated with functionality and awareness components;
- only two topics of FLE, out of sixteen topics were introduced in two of the NAEP primers, viz., family size and health and nutritional needs of family;
- both the topics had illustrations which were relevant to the content; and
- there was no specific sequence, pattern or order in introducing FLE content within the primer or primer to primer.

The perspective of the FLE content in the NAEP primers is as follows :

- The topic 8, "What happens when Population Increases" (*Janam Perigithe Emavuthundo Thelusa*) of primer 1 explains the problems of over population through non-verbal messages, independent words, sentences and slogans. The non-verbal message conveyed through illustration was that, larger families which were economically poor were unable to provide adequate food to their children. This message was explained through a picture, in which a poor family consisting of a sad faced couple and five children, who were crying due to hunger and empty vessels around without food.
- In another message, namely, "Over population places more demand on facilities available", a picture in which a over crowded bus and a long queue of women awaiting for water near a tube well were depicted. Thus the topic 8 of primer 1 introduced a part of the FLE content related to family size and the importance of small family. Similarly, topic 7, "To be healthy" (*Arogyamga Vundalante*) of primer 3 explains the importance of Health and Nutrition through a story, illustrations, independent words and sentences.

- The content of topic 7 focuses more on the importance of immunization, immunization schedule, protected water, and the need for eating good food. This was explained in the form of a story in which a couple take their sick child to a doctor who explains the information related to the topics mentioned above. The messages conveyed through the illustrations were slightly different from the content explained through a story. The illustrations were about a small family in which the father was reading a newspaper and children were discussing something while looking at a book and the mother was preparing a meal. The following illustrations were made to highlight the importance of balanced diet :
  - picture of balanced diet consisting of different foods grouped into four groups;
  - mothers with children in their arms were standing in queue in a health centre, where a doctor was immunizing a child;
  - the doctor was testing a man in a primary health centre, while a woman with a boy at her side was overlooking them.

Thus, the topic 7 of primer 3, introduced as a part of the FLE content related to the topic on Health and Nutritional Needs of a Family.

The content covered in NAEP primers was not adequate as it has introduced only a part of the two topics of the FLE content identified. The content promotes awareness and knowledge but does not promote understanding, attitudes, practices and skills related to FLE. For adequate coverage of FLE content and to educate adolescent girl participants of NAEP, there is a need to develop a separate curriculum in the form of a manual to promote knowledge, understanding, attitudes, practices and skills related to FLE.

Besides the NAEP primers, the guidance manual (*Volunteerlaku Suchanalu*) of NAEP IPCL materials which serves as a guide to the volunteers/animators who impart education to the participants of adult education programme was also examined for FLE content. The manual gives the following details for every topic in each primer:

- showing the picture the animator should raise the following questions;
- description of picture;

- things to be given though;
- information.

The examination of the instructions given in the Manual for topic 8 in primer 1, throws light on topics 4, 6, 9, 13 and 15 of FLE, i.e., family responsibilities, family size, management of family resources, family planning methods and good parenting practices. A few independent statements related to the above said topics were made in the form of sentences. Directions to volunteers were given to initiate discussions related to topics 4 and 9. In the description of the illustrations information related to topics 4 and 8 were mentioned. None of the above said FLE topics were covered adequately. The information covered does not promote understanding, attitudes, practices and skills related to the topics, but an attempt was made to create an awareness.

The topic 7 in primer 3, to some extent covers the topic on Health and Nutritional Needs. Information on balanced diet, immunization and hygiene were included in the form of questions (to be raised by the volunteer in the session), description of illustrations and also the information about the topic. Yet, the content covered was not adequate. The content included creates an awareness and promotes knowledge to some extent. But Exercises to promote understanding, attitudes, practices and skills were not included.

Based on the findings of content analysis of NAEP primers and FLE needs of adolescent girls (as perceived by experts, married women and unmarried girls), a manual was drafted to serve as a practical resource guide for animators who are intended to be involved in teaching/training/communicating family life education concepts.

FLE Manual

The manual consisted of an introduction conceptual frame work lessons and evaluation schedules. The conceptual frame work presents the FLE content into seven important and appropriate units.

Family;
Family Roles and Responsibilities;
Family Life Cycle;
Family Needs and Resources;
Marriage;

Parenthood; and
Family Welfare Services.

All the sixteen topics (identified) were grouped under these 7 units. The lessons were planned for the topics deriving the information from various resource material—manual, handbooks, reports and other forms of curriculum materials that have been prepared in India, Philippines, Malaysia and Some Western Countries, for use in their respective family life education programmes.

As the volunteers/instructors were familiar with the pattern followed in the guidance manual of IPCL primers, it was taken as a model for developing lessons. For every lesson, illustrations were designed and an evaluation sheet consisting of ten questions were developed to assess the impact of the FLE programme. In all the sixteen lessons, the presentation of content was described under the following six dimensions.

1. *Showing the Picture the Animator should Raise the Following Questions*

Relevant questions pertaining to the illustrations were framed to gather already known information (about the topic) from the participants. This helps the participants to identify the characters/situations given in the picture and to recall their knowledge and past experiences related to the picture.

2. *Description of Picture*

The situations illustrated in the picture were described adequately to ensure proper understanding of the picture.

3. *Things to be given thought*

This dimension generates few thought provoking questions relevant to the topic to initiate thinking and better participation.

4. *Information*

The conceptual and theoretical issues relevant to the topic were presented meaningfully in this dimension.

5. *Suggested activity*

To reinforce the information imparted and to promote better understanding an activity was suggested, which is to be monitored by the animator involving all the participants using participatory technique.

FLEP Evaluation Schedule

To assess the FLE programme, a structured questionnaire consisting of 160 questions (i.e., 10 questions on each topic) along with scoring key was framed.

Table 4.17
The Mean Initial Knowledge Scores of Unmarried Adolescent Girls

S. No.	*FLE Topics*	*No. of participants*	*Mean*	*Standard deviation*
1.	Concept of Family	30	4.267	2.083
2.	Family Functions	30	3.667	3.726
3.	Family Roles and Relationships	30	1.433	2.269
4.	Family Responsibilities	30	1.467	2.300
5.	Family Life Cycle	30	1.267	0.450
6.	Family Size	30	0.200	0.484
7.	Health and Nutritional Needs of Family	30	0.900	1.062
8.	Psycho-social Needs of Family	30	1.533	1.548
9.	Management of Family Resources	30	2.400	1.248
10.	Menstruation and Changes in the Body	30	1.500	0.974
11.	Mate Selection	30	1.862	0.860
12.	Pregnancy and Child Birth	30	1.467	0.681
13.	Family Planning	30	1.033	0.669
14.	Care of Children	30	1.467	0.937
15.	Good Parenting Practices	30	0.833	0.746
16.	Family Welfare Services	30	0.167	0.379
	Total	30	25.470	16.460

Impact of FLE Programme on NAEP Participants

The curriculum thus developed was field tested on a sample of thirty unmarried adolescent girls who were participants on Non-formal Adult Education Programme. The FLEP was carried out for a period of 3 months and the FLE knowledge of the sample before and after the programme was evaluated.

FLE Knowledge of the NAEP Participants Before and After the FLE Programme

The mean and standard deviations of initial and final knowledge scores of unmarried adolescent girls are presented in Tables 4.17 and 4.18.

Table 4.18
The Mean Final Knowledge Scores of Unmarried Adolescent Girls

S. No.	*FLE Topics*	*No. of participants*	*Mean*	*Standard deviation*
1.	Concept of Family	30	9.633	0.615
2.	Family Functions	30	9.633	0.616
3.	Family Roles and Relationships	30	9.400	0.724
4.	Family Responsibilities	30	9.100	0.995
5.	Family Life Cycle	30	9.200	0.997
6.	Family Size	30	9.667	0.547
7.	Health and Nutritional Needs of Family	30	9.433	0.626
8.	Psycho-social Needs of Family	30	9.433	0.568
9.	Management of Family Resources	30	9.367	0.615
10.	Menstruation and Changes in the Body	30	9.133	0.819
11.	Mate Selection	30	9.367	0.765
12.	Pregnancy and Child Birth	30	9.233	0.679
13.	Family Planning	30	9.133	0.571
14.	Care of Children	30	9.233	0.728
15.	Good Parenting Practices	30	8.967	0.615
16.	Family Welfare Services	30	8.700	0.651
	Total	30	148.600	5.9860

Table 4.17 reveals that the average initial knowledge scores were less than 1 for four topics and less than 2 for ten topics. For the first two topics, the mean score was around 4. This shows that the sample had very low knowledge of all topics except for the first two, which were familiar topics, viz., concept of family and functions of family.

The mean final knowledge scores of unmarried adolescent girls (given in Table 4.18, shows that the mean scores were above 9 for 14 topics and around 8 for 2 topics.

The scores show that there had been a significant improvement in the FLE knowledge of adolescent girls, after the family life education programme. This shows that the learning activities framed in the FLE manual had a significant effect on the learners and the manual was found to be beneficial and suitable as a resource guide for the FLE programme organisers.

Impact of FLE Programme on NAEP Participants

To study the impact of family life education programme on unmarried adolescent girls, "paired t" test was used for final and initial knowledge scores. The findings are presented in Table 4.19.

Table 4.19
"t" Values for Final-Initial Knowledge Scores

S. No.	*FLE Topics*	*'t' Value*
1.	Concept of Family	13.94**
2.	Family Functions	9.06**
3.	Family Roles and Relationships	20.08**
4.	Family Responsibilities	21.00**
5.	Family Life Cycle	46.01**
6.	Family Size	71.06**
7.	Health and Nutritional Needs of Family	40.06**
8.	Psycho-social Needs of Family	31.51**
9.	Management of Family Resources	33.80**
10.	Menstruation and Changes in the Body	51.70**
11.	Mate Selection	52.88**
12.	Pregnancy and Child Birth	54.77**
13.	Family Planning	62.31**
14.	Care of Children	54.97**
15.	Good Parenting Practices	61.00**
16.	Family Welfare Services	68.59**

Notes : *Significant at 0.05 level.**Signficant at 0.01 level.

It can be observed that the calculated value of 't' is higher than the table value at 0.01 level for all the topics. Hence, the results of the experiment provide evidence in favour of the stated hypothesis. Therefore, it can be concluded that the FLE Manual is highly suitable for FLE programme and the FLEP was found to have an impact on the unmarried adolescent participants.

5

Summary and Conclusion

Introduction

Family Life Education is a relatively new concept. It aims at promoting the quality of life through responsible decision making and improved understanding of human relationships and family roles. The term FLE has different meanings ranging from the narrow concept of education in family planning to the broader notion of education for leading a healthy, purposeful and constructive life. In a developing country like India where conditions of poverty and ignorance are rampant and where the pressures and strains of life relate to mobilising the basic resources necessary for mere existence, the concept of FLE assumes different ramifications. FLE in its broadest sense, includes all educational efforts designed to prepare people at any stage to make the most of family living. A well integrated programme of FLE could help families adopt themselves to new changes and assume greater responsibility for the transformation of society.

The National Council of Family Relations of America (NCFRA) stated that FLE is intended "To guide individuals and families in improving their interpersonal relationships and furthering their maximum development". In addition, the council stated that FLE programmes "Seek to improve their quality of life throughout the entire range of human development". The range includes physical and emotional growth, individual and sexual development, dating and courtship, marriage and parenthood. It continuously emphasizes the importance of personal integrity and family responsibility (Smith, 1970). However, some extra dimensions are added to the range described above such as, the physical, socio-psychological growth and sexual development, pre-marriage preparation, marriage, parenthood and spirituality of the members of the family. India being a technologically developing country, areas such as environmental and personal hygiene, preventive health and nutrition are to be woven in to the programme content (Gokarn, 1986).

FLE as a formally structured intervention to help members of the family, has been practised for over a few decades. Yet even today, "What FLE is"? and "What FLE ought to be" ?, remain the subject of a continuing debate. It is, however, accepted that the FLE approach is both preventive and developmental, and is directed "To teach" people to "Live together", creatively and with affection in the family. With respect to the theoretical under pinnings of the FLE, there is no fully accepted single frame of reference. Hence, any frame considered should be viewed as open and liable to additions and modifications.

FLE is perceived to be usually operating through non-formal education which incidentally everyone receives. Many programmes have been conceived and implemented in India for extension education of women using non-formal approach. Notably, FLE was an important constituent of most of them. Yet, in actual implementation, no programme provides FLE except Grihini training programme, which were intended for Tribal girls in Bihar, Madhya Pradesh, West Bengal, Orissa and Maharashtra (Kapoor, 1986). The factors responsible for the activities of FLE not being conducted in the spirit and to the extent they should be, were revealed in a study conducted by Kapoor (1986). The factors were three fold; first, the factors that relate to the physical facilities available and the third, those that concern the supervision and guidance given to field level functionaries. This indicates that there is a great need to reinforce and strengthen the existing extension education programmes in order to impart FLE to the needy groups.

Family Planning Association of India (FPAI), a National Voluntary organisation founded in 1949 in Bombay, has done pioneering work in the area of FLE. The FPAI integrated family life issues with population education components in their educational programmes organised for adolescents and adults. Sporadic efforts have been made to introduce FLE in the formal schools by FPAI. But noteworthy efforts were not made in the non-formal sector.

FLE as a developing subject levels a definite content,

approach and a channel for introduction. A review of existing literature of FLE in India and survey of existing Governmental and Non-governmental programmes having objectives relevant to FLE, revealed that.

- non-formal adult education programme as a nationwide activity covering adolescents and adults, stressing the values of cooperation, equality and group solidarity is highly suitable as channel for introducing FLE to adolescents;
- there is a need to identify FLE content based on the perceptions of intended learners themselves and experts;
- an examination of existing curriculum of NAEP for FLE content and the extent of its coverage; and
- development of curriculum on the basis of perceived needs and inadequacies in the existing NAEP curriculum and testing its impact on the intended learners.

Hence, non-formal adult education programme with a well developed infrastructure was found to be ideal for reaching the illiterate adolescent girls. The present study aims at utilising this NFAE programme for imparting family life education. FLE as part of non-formal adult education programme can assist the unreached young generation in strengthening their family lives.

Statement of the Problem

Family life education for the unmarried adolescent girls through the non-formal adult education programme.

Objectives of the Study

The major objectives of the study were :

- Identification of the FLE needs of adolescent learners of NFAEP as perceived by the learners themselves; married adult women and the subject experts.
- Assessment of the factors causing differential perceptions about FLE needs of adolescent learners by married adult women, experts and unmarried adolescent girls.
- To assess the impact of age, family income, caste, type of family size of the family and marital status on FLE need perception of unmarried adolescent learners of NFAEP.
- Examination of the adequacy and relevance of FLE content in the NFAEP.

- Development of a model FLE curriculum for unmarried adolescent girls.
- Evaluation of the effectiveness of model FLE curriculum for adolescent girls.

Hypotheses

In order to accomplish the foregoing objectives, the following hypotheses were formulated :

- the FLE need perception of adolescent girls, married adult women and subject experts is significantly different from each other;
- the FLE need perception of adolescent girls and married adult women is significantly influenced by their socio-economic background;
- the coverage of FLE information in NFAEP primers is not adequate;
- a need based curriculum has a significant impact on the FLE status of unmarried adolescent girls.

Research Design

Participatory action research method was used. It is a means of utilising knowledge and research to institute change and at the same time establishing an integrated relationship between theory and life.

Locale of the Study

The Chittoor district in Andhra Pradesh was selected purposively for the following reasons:

- the researcher hails from the Chittoor district and, therefore, it is ideally suited to undertake participatory action research in the district;
- the Chittoor district is the representative backward district of the State in terms of the distribution of rural and urban population, degree of female literacy and other socio-economic parameters;
- special adult education programmes were launched in the district under Total Literacy Campaign (TLC); and
- separate NAEP primers were exclusively prepared for this district and field tested.

Sample Selection

The area of study was Chittoor district. Multistage random sampling procedure was used for the selection of sample from the 66 Mandals of Chittoor district. In the first instance, 5 rural and 5 urban mandals were selected using Tippets random sampling technique. From each mandal 5 villages/areas were selected and from each village 2 married women aged between 20-30 years and 8 adolescent girls aged between 13-19 years were selected. Thus, a sample of 500 NFAEP learners were selected for the study. Out of 500 subjects, 100 were married women, aged between 20-30 years. The remaining 400 were unmarried adolescent girls.

Variables

In this study, family life education needs were the dependent variables and the major independent variables were age, family income, caste, type of family and marital status.

Tools of the Study

The following tools were employed in the study :

FLE needs identification scale English and Telugu;
General information schedule;
Tool for FLE content analysis;
FLE curriculum; and
FLE programme evaluation schedules.

Assessment of Variables

FLE needs of adolescent girls identified by experts, married women and unmarried girls were ranked on the basis of the mean scores obtained for each topic, in each group. The topics ranked high in all the groups were chosen for inclusion in FLE curriculum.

On the basis of topics identified for FLE, the content analysis of non-formal adult education programme primers of Chittoor District was done. Based on the findings of content analysis of NFAEP primers and FLE needs of adolescent learners (as perceived by experts, married women and unmarried girls) a manual was prepared to serve as a practical resource guide for animators/ volunteers, who are intended to be involved in teaching/training/ communicating FLE. Client-oriented and expert oriented approaches were used in development of FLE curriculum to ensure better participation of learners. The Manual was field tested on a sample of thirty adolescent girls, who were participants in NFAEP. The FLE knowledge of the sample before and after the education programme was evaluated. The impact of FLE programme on adolescent learners was assessed.

Statistical Analysis of Data

Both qualitative and quantitative analysis of data were attempted. Qualitative analysis consisted of content analysis of NFAEP primers. Further, chi-square test was used to study the association of independent variables with the perception of FLE needs. Mean and standard deviation of initial/final knowledge scores of adolescent learners for each topic was also computed. A paired 't' test was used to study the impact of FLE programme on adolescent learners.

Salient Findings

The data on respondents' exposure to FLE information revealed that :

- only 23 per cent of the total respondents had opportunities to know FLE information;
- the sources for knowing FLE information were AEP, parents and elders, friends and mass media;
- only 7.8 per cent of the respondents utilised the FLE information known to them;
- out of 500 married and unmarried respondents, only 9.2 per cent made special effort to know and practise FLE information.
- the data on the sources/persons which were helpful to the respondents in their special effort to know and practise FLE information showed that the mass media was assigned first rank. Friends as a source was accorded second and third rank, parents and elders were assigned second and third rank respectively. Ranking trend revealed that the mass media was most helpful to the respondents to acquire and practise FLE information;
- of the total respondents only 1.2 per cent stated that they were informed about FLE in AEP;
- a negligible per cent (0.2) of the respondents expressed their

satisfaction with the FLE information imparted in AEP;

- majority of the respondents (75.6 per cent) felt that there was need for more FLE information to be taught in AEP;
- 81.6 per cent of the total respondents felt the need for FLE information in the form of a book;
- only 2.2 per cent of the total respondents had opportunities to see illustrations related to FLE and could read some information such as, titles, captions and independent words published in printed media such as, Telugu news papers and magazines;
- almost all the respondents listened to the Radio. Yet, only 4.8 per cent had opportunities to listen to FLE information broadcast in Telugu, through All India Radio;
- the largest number of cinema are produced in Telugu language. Of the total respondents, 15.8 per cent had opportunities to view FLE related information in Telugu cinema. The distribution of the respondents according to the number of cinema in which they have seen FLE information showed that unmarried adolescent girls viewed more cinema than married adult women and urban respondents viewed comparatively more number of cinemas than their rural counterparts;
- the data on respondents' exposure to FLE information disseminated through film shows showed that 8.4 per cent of the total respondents had opportunities to view film shows related to FLE. Of these the percentage of unmarried adolescent girls were more than the married adult women. The number of film shows viewed, for all the respondents were less than five. This shows that the number of film shows shown and the coverage of population was very small;
- in spite of T.V., being a popular mass media, only 33.2 per cent of the total respondents had opportunities to view FLE related information telecast through Doordarshan. The frequency of exposure to FLE related programmes telecast was also very small. This could be due to inaccessibility to T.V. sets to a majority of households. Besides, the inappropriate telecast schedule and urban and elite orientation of the T.V., programmes have alienated some of those respondents who had T.V. facility;
- the information gathered on the content of the FLE information, to which the respondents were exposed revealed that, the information was mostly related to the topics family

size, family planning methods, family welfare services, concept of family and family life cycle. The information received by the respondents through various sources were not holistic, systematic and consistent. This shows that there is great need to extend FLE information to the needy groups; and

- FLE needs of unmarried adolescent girls identified by experts, married women and unmarried adolescent girls were ranked based on the mean scores obtained for each topic in each group. The topics ranked high in all the three groups were chosen for inclusion in FLE curriculum, thus 16 topics were identified. They were:

  - Concept of family;
  - Family functions;
  - Family roles and relationships;
  - Family responsibilities;
  - Family life cycle;
  - Family size;
  - Health and nutritional needs;
  - Psycho-social needs of family;
  - Management of family resources;
  - Menstruation and changes in the body;
  - Mate selection;
  - Pregnancy and child birth;
  - Family planning methods;
  - Care of children;
  - Good parenting practices; and
  - Family welfare services.

The strength of preference of experts was relatively high for the first 12 topics (a mean score of 3.0), followed by topics 13 and 14 (mean scores of 2.7 and 2.3, respectively). The experts assigned lower ranks to topics 15 and 16 (mean scores of 1.8 and 1.7, respectively) on the other hand. The married women exhibited highest preference to first 8 topics and 10th topic (mean scores ranged between 2.5 and 2.7), next preferred topics were 9, 15, 16, 11 and 12 (mean scores falling between 2.0 to 2.4) and lowest preference was accorded to topics 13 and 14 (mean scores 1.9 and 1.8, respectively).

The mean preferences exhibited by unmarried adolescent girls were relatively high for the topics 1, 2 and 5 (mean scores varied between 2.5 and 2.6). The next preferred topics were 3, 6, 8,

15 (a mean score of 2.4) followed by topics 7, 11, 16, 4, 10, 12, 9 and 13 (mean scores ranged between 2.1 and 2.4) whereas lowest preference was given to topic 14 (a mean score of 1.8).

From the foregoing, it is evident that the experts exhibited highest preference for the majority of the topics (14 topics): In comparison with unmarried adolescent girls, the married adult women assigned higher scores for majority of the topics. This could be because the experts and married women viewed the topics as more important due to their exposure and experience. The data also reveals that there was variation in preferences exhibited by the three groups.

Impact of socio-economic background of married women and unmarried adolescent girls on FLE need perception were studied by examining the association of independent variables such as age, caste, type of family, family income and marital status on perception of FLE needs.

- Age was not significantly associated with the perception of FLE needs of married women of two age groups. In the case of unmarried adolescent girls, significant difference was found for three topics and for the 13 topics no significant association was found between age and FLE perception. This difference between married women and unmarried girls may be attributed to their marital status;
- the chi-square values of married women for all the 16 topics showed that there is no significant difference between the income groups and their perception of FLE needs. In the case of unmarried girls, significant difference was found between the income groups for 11 topics and no significant difference was found between the income groups for 5 topics. This shows that family income influences perception of FLE needs in unmarried girls. Similar influences were not found to exist in married women. This may be attributed to their marital status;
- Caste was not significantly associated with the perception of FLE needs of married women. In the case of unmarried adolescent girls significant difference was found between caste and perception of FLE needs for only 3 topics and for remaining 13 topics no significant difference was found. This difference between married women and unmarried girls may be due to their marital status;
- No significant difference was found between the type of family and perception of FLE needs among married women.

In the case of unmarried girls significant difference was found for only two topics and no significant difference was found for remaining 14 topics;

- The perceived FLE needs of married women and unmarried girls was significantly associated with their marital status for 14 topics and for the remaining two topics significant difference was not found.

The analysis of FAEP Primer (1990) of Chittoor district revealed that :

- a very small portion of FLE content integrated in two of the NAEP primers (Text 1 and 3);
- the FLE content was introduced in topic 8 of primer I and topic 7 of primer III, in the form of independent words, sentences, non-verbal messages (illustrations), slogans and story. In both the topics (8 and 7) FLE content was integrated with functionality and awareness components;
- the FLE content introduced in NAEP primers was related to the two topics, "Family Size" and "Health and Nutritional Needs of a Family" of the sixteen topics identified under the present study;
- there was no specific sequence, pattern or order in introducing FLE content within the primer or primer to primer;
- the FLE content covered in NAEP primers was not adequate, as only a part of the two topics of the FLE content identified was introduced;
- the content covered promotes awareness and knowledge, but does not promote understanding, attitudes, practices or skills related to FLE; and
- for adequate coverage of FLE content and to educate adolescent girls participants of NAEP, there is a need to develop a separate curriculum in the form of a manual to promote knowledge, understanding, attitudes, practices and skills related to FLE.

Development of Family Life Education Manual

A need based FLE curriculum in the form of a manual was drafted to serve as a practical resource guide for animators of NAEP who are intended to be involved in FLE programme. The manual consisted of 16 topics identified by experts, married women and unmarried adolescent girls. The topics were grouped under 7 units. The existing NAEP instructors manual (*Instructions to Volunteers*) was taken as a model for developing lessons, as the animators/ instructors were familiar with the pattern followed. The FLE manual consisted of introduction, lessons and evaluation schedules.

The curriculum developed was field tested on a sample of thirty unmarried adolescent girls, who were participants of Non-formal Adult Education programme. The FLE knowledge of the sample before and after the programme was evaluated. The mean initial knowledge scores of the sample was low on all the topics except for the first two, which were familiar topics, viz., concept of family and family functions. The mean final knowledge score of unmarried adolescent girls showed that the mean scores were above 9 (out of 10) for 14 topics and around 8 for 2 topics which indicates that there is a significant improvement in the FLE knowledge of adolescent girls, after the FLE programme.

To know the impact of FLE programme on NAEP participants the t-test as used to assess the significance of difference between final and initial knowledge scores. The findings showed that there was significant difference between the initial and final knowledge mean scores at 0.01 level. Therefore, it can be concluded that the FLE programme had an impact on the sample and the FLE curriculum developed in the form of a manual was beneficial to the unmarried adolescent girl participants of NAEP.

Conclusion

The study leads to the conclusion that adolescent girls need to be imparted Family Life Education. Despite the differences in the perception of FLE needs by subject experts, married adult women and unmarried adolescent girls, the scores assigned by the three groups for the majority of the topics (identified) ranged between 2 and 3 meaning thereby that the three groups perceived the need for FLE and identified the content areas (16 topics) for inclusion in FLE curriculum.

The study revealed that the major source of FLE related information was mass media and that friends, parents and elders and the organised Adult Education Programme played a negligible role in providing FLE information to the respondents. Majority of the respondents felt the need for publication and distribution of FLE information in the form of a book. As the respondents were neoliterates, their reading abilities were probably not sufficient to understand the FLE information printed in the form of a book.

Development of FLE curriculum in the form of a manual, to impart FLE through NFAEP—a nationwide programme covering adolescents and adults is found to be highly suitable channel for introducing FLE.

The independent variables of age, family income, caste, type of family were not significantly associated with the perception of FLE needs of married women. But these independent variables were found to be associated with perception of FLE needs of unmarried adolescent girls for few topics. Marital status, as an independent variable was found to be significantly associated with perception of FLE needs of both the groups, i.e., married and unmarried. This could be due to the differences in the exposure, experience and sexual maturity between the two groups. Hence it can be concluded that except marital status, other independent variables included in the present study did not have much influence on the FLE needs perception of the respondents.

The FLE content covered in NAEP primers was found to be not adequate. For adequate coverage of FLE content and to educate unmarried adolescent girl participants of NAEP, there is a need for developing a separate curriculum in the form of a manual to promote knowledge, understanding, attitudes, practices and skills related to FLE.

The study further established that the FLE curriculum developed, based on the perceived needs of the three groups, viz., experts, married adult women and unmarried adolescent girls had a significant effect on the selected NAEP learners on whom the curriculum was field tested through an FLE programme. The FLE programme had improved the FLE knowledge of the participants significantly. The curriculum developed in the form of a manual appears to be highly suitable for imparting FLE through NAEP.

Bibliography

Acchpal, B. and Verma, A., 1988. Towards Better Families : An Integrated Approach to Family Life Education and Family Welfare, Baroda.

Adams, B.C., 1985. A Study of the relationship between 6th grades: Physical, Social and Cognitive development and the acquisition of knowledge in a sex education programme. Dissertation Abstract International, 46 : 57(A).

Aldous, J., 1978. Family Careers Developmental Change in Families. New York, John Wiley.

Amato, R.P., 1993. Family Structure, Family Process, and Family Ideology. The Journal of Marriage and the Family, 55 (1), 50-53.

Audinarayana, N., 1985. Interrelationship Between Socio-economic Variables and Age at Marriage. Journal of Family Welfare, Vol. (4) 39-45.

Augustine, J.S., 1982. The Indian Family in Transition. Delhi, Vikas Publishing House Pvt. Ltd., 41-93.

Balu, R., 1989. Family Life Education in Aided School. The Indian Journal of Social Work, L(4), 497-504.

Bank, L., Forgatch, S.M., Patterson, R.G. and Fetrow, A.R., 1993. Parenting Practices of Single Mothers : Mediators of Negative Contextual Factors. Journal of Marriage and the Family, 55, 371-83.

Benedict, 1938. Cited by Llyod, A.M. (1985) in Adolescence. New York, Harper and Row Publishers, 4-61.

Bhatia, S.C. and Mehta, M.L., 1985. Development Oriented Adult Education, New Delhi, IUACE, 56-57.

Billimoria, J., Bhattacharya, R. and Datar, C., 1993. New Methods of Continuing Family Life Development Programmes. The Indian Journal of Social Work, TISS. Bombay, 54 (1), 47-57.

Boulby, J., 1951. Maternal Care and Mental Health. Geneva, World Health Organisation.

Boone, J.E., 1985. Developing Programmes in Adult Education. Englewood Cliffs, Prentice Hall Inc.

Bron Fenbrenner, V., 1986. Ecology of the Family as a Context for Human Development: Research Perspectives. Developmental Psychology 22, 723-42.

Bulcroft, A.R. and Bulcroft, A.K., 1992. Race Differences in Attitudinal and Motivational Factors in the Decision to Marry. Journal of Marriage and the Family, 55, 338-55.

CBCI Commission, 1975. The Family and Laity Training Course in Family Apostolate. Family Life Education Course for VII, VIII, IX, and X standard.

Cox, S.H., 1970. Intra Family Comparison of Loving—Rejecting Child-Rearing Practices. Child Devleopment, 41, 437-48.

Dang, H. and Aggarwal, J.C., 1986. Implementation of the New Education Policy—A Critical Evaluation of the Programme of Action. New Delhi, Arya Book Depot, 1-24.

Dave, C. and Sadashivaiah, K., 1981. Family Size and Quality of Life, Social Change, 11 (3 and 4), 35-44.

Datta, S.C., 1987. Adult Education in Third World. New Delhi, Criterion Publications.

Deacon, E.R. and Firebaugh, M.F., 1981. Family Resource Management. Boston, Allyn and Bacon, 52, 75-84.

Deal, J.E., Halverson, C.F. Jr. and Wampler, K.S., 1989. Parental Agreement on Child Rearing Orientation, Relations to Parental, Marital, Family and Child Characteristics. Child Development, 60, 1025-34.

Desai, 1956. Cited by Goode, W.J. (1987) in the Family (2nd ed). New Delhi, Prentice Hall of India Pvt. Ltd.

Desai, M., 1993. Family Dynamics and Developmental Programmes: Curriculum Planning. The Indian Journal of Social Work, 54(1), 3-21.

Desai, M., 1993. Marital Dynamics and Developmental Programmes. The Indian Journal of Social Work, 54(1), 70-84.

Desai, M., 1993. Selection of Marriage Partner and Developmental Programmes. The Indian Journal of Social Work, 54(1).

Dubois, L.D., Eitel, K.S. and Felner, D.R., 1994. Effects of Family Environment and Parent Child Relationships on School Adjustment During the Transition to Early Adolescence. Journal of Marriage and the Family, 56(2), 405-14.

Duke, C., 1988. Adult Education and Poverty : What are the Connections. Adult Education and Development, 30, 38-49.

Dunhan, C.C. and Bengtson, L.V., 1994. Married with Children : Protest and the Timing of Family Course Events. Journal of Marriage and the Family, 56, 224-28.

Erikson, E.H., 1950. Cited by Lloyd, A.M. (1985) in Adolescence. New York, Harper and Row Publishers.

Erikson, E.H., 1958. Cited by Rao, P.M. (1988) in Adolescence—A Perspective and a Need for Family Life Education. The Journal of Family Welfare, 35(2), 42-47.

Fosset, A.M. and Kiecolt, J.T., 1993. Mate Availability and Family Structure among African Americans in US Metropolitan Area. Journal of Marriage and the Family, 55(2), 288-302.

Gangrade, K.D., 1975. Crisis of Values : A Study on Generation Gap, New Delhi, Chetna Publications.

Gangrade, K.D. and Singh, R. 1992. Community Approach to Family Planning Education. IASSI Quarterly, 2(2), 90-95.

Garg and Parikh, 1976. Cited by Kashyap, D.L.C. (1993) in Adolescent/Youth and Family Dynamics and Development Programmes. The Indian Journal of Social Work, 54(1) : 92-105.

Garrett, E.G. and Woodworth, S.R., 1981. Statistics in Psychology and Education. Bombay, Vakils, Feffer and Simons Ltd.

Gelles, R.J., 1974. Cited by Goode, W.J. (1987) in The Family (2nd ed). New Delhi, Prentice Hall of India Pvt. Ltd.

Gesell, A., 1956. Cited by Lloyd, A.M. (1985) in Adolescence. New York, Harper and Row Publishers, 4-61.

Gold Thorpe, J.E., 1989. Family Life in Western Societies—A Historical Sociology of Family Relationships in Britain and North America. Cambridge, Cambridge University Press, 46-55.

Goode, W.J., 1987. The Family (2nd Ed.). New Delhi, Prentice Hall of India Pvt. Ltd.

Gore, M.S., 1968. Urbanisation and Family Change in India, Bombay, Popular Prakasam.

Gopalan, C. and Kaur, S., 1989. Women and Nutrition in India, New Delhi, NFI.

Gopalan, C., 1992. Health and Nutritional Status of India's Children and Women : Suggested Strategies for Rapid Improvement. IASSI Quarterly, 2(2), 36-41.

Government of A.P., 1990. Handout of Enriched ICDS Project in 110 Blocks of 13 districts of A.P.

Griffin, C., 1987. Adult Education : As Social Policy. London, Croom Helm.

Gupta, N.L., 1988. New Education Policy : A New Era in Education. Ajmer, Krishna Brothers.

Gupta, R., Gupta, U. and Gupta, K.B., 1989. Education for Responsible Parenthood. Social Welfare, 39(4-5), 17-19.

Freud, A., 1937. Cited by Lloyd, A.M. (1985) in Adolescence. New York, Harper and Row Publishers, 4-61.

Freud, A., 1969. Cited by Rao, P.M. (1988) in Adolescence—A Perspective and a Need for Family Life Education, The Journal of Family Welfare, 35(2) : 42-47.

Hall, G.S., 1920. Cited by Lloyd, A.M. (1985) in Adolescence. New York, Harper and Row Publishers, 4-61.

Hahn, A.B., 1993. Marital Status and Women's Health : The Effect of Economic Marital Acquisitions. Journal of Marriage and the Family, 55, 494-504.

Haxton, P.D., 1984. Development as if Children Mattered. New Delhi, UNICEF.

Hogan, D.P., 1987. Demographic Trends in Human Fertility and Parenting Across the Life Span.

Indian Universities Association for Continuing Education, 1990. Discussion Support Document on Age at Marriage. Delhi.

Pilai, S.I. and Ranjinidevi, G.S., 1992. Decision Making in the Home. Social Welfare, 39(3), 23-26.

Jain, S. and Shivpuri, V., 1993. Education for Better Living of Rural Adolescent Girls. Training Modules, Social Awareness, 2.

Jain A., 1991. Mobilisation of Women Through Educational Training Camps. Journal of Education and Social Change, 4(4), 77-92.

Jena, Basantibala and Rabindranath, P., 1989. Health and Family Welfare Services in India. New Delhi, Ashish Publishing House.

Jesudasan, V., Roy, P. and Koshy, T.A., 1981. Non-formal Education for Rural Women to Promote the Development of the Young Child. New Delhi, Allied Publishers Pvt. Ltd.

Johnson, B.M., Shulman, S. and Collins, W.A., 1991. Systematic Patterns of Parenting as reported by Adolescents; Devleopmental Differences and Implications for Psychosocial Outcomes. Journal of Adolescent Research, 6, 235-52.

Joseph, P.J., 1973. Cited by Rao, P.M. (1988) in Adolescence—A Perspective and a Need for Family Life Education. The Journal of Family Welfare, 35(2): 42-47.

Kapadia, 1972. Cited by Goode, W.J. (1987) in The Family (2nd Ed). New Delhi, Prentice Hall of India Pvt. Ltd.

Kapoor, M., 1986. Women and Family Life Education in India. Jaipur, Printwell Publishers.

Kashyap. L., 1993. Family Interactions. The Indian Journal of Social Work, 54(1), 22-29.

Khan, H.A., 1989. Simulation: A Realistic Technique in Teacher Education. Journal of Indian Education, 15(1).

Kolenda, P., 1987. Regional Differences in Family Structure in India, Jaipur, Rawat Publications.

Koshy, T.A., 1973. Integrated Non-formal Education for Mothers. Social Change, 3(1-2), 28-32.

Keet, S.M., 1981. Family Care—How to Look After Yourself and Your Family. London, The Macmillan Press Ltd.

Kumar, R., 1988. Child Development in India—Health Welfare and Management (Vol. 1). New Delhi, Ashish Publishing House, 64-97.

Kundu, C.L., 1984. Adult Education Principles, Practice and Prospects. New Delhi, Sterling Publishers Pvt. Ltd.

Kulkarni, S., 1988. Parent Education. Perspectives and Approaches. Jaipur, Rawat Publications.

Kurian, G., 1981. Some Changing Trends in Mate Selection and Marriage. Indian Journal of Social Research, 22(2), 172-82.

Lakshmidevi, A., 1988. Rural Women Management in Farm and Home. New Delhi, Northern Book Centre.

Laslett, P., 1977. Family Life and Illicit Love in Earlier Generations : Essays in Historical Sociology. Cambridge, Cambridge University Press.

Leslie, G.R. and Korman, S.K., 1984. The Family in Social Context, New York, Oxford University Press.

Lloyd, A.M., 1985. Adolescence. New York, Harper and Row Publishers, 4-61.

Lustern, T.. Boger, R. and Hanman, K., 1993. Infant Affect and Home Environment. Journal of Marriage and the Family, 55, 651-61.

Mahale, N.M., 1987. The Adolescents—Their Family Situations and Education. Delhi, Mittal Publications.

Mane, P., 1993. Understanding and Enhancing Family Communications. The Indian Journal of Social Work, 54(1), 32-43.

Madan, G.R., 1987. Indian Social Problems—Social Disorganisation and Reconstruction (Vol. II). Allied Publishers Pvt. Ltd.

Mali, M.G., 1984. Adult Education in India, Deep and Deep Publications.

Mani, G., 1984. Designing Curriculum for Non-formal and Adult Education, in Reddy, M.M. and Ravi Sankar, S. (Eds.). Curriculum Development and Educational Technological. New Delhi, Sterling Publishers Pvt. Ltd., 53-76.

Mascarenhas, M.M., 1986. Family Life Education Value Education. Bangalore, CREST.

Mathai, T.S., 1993. Education for Better Living of Rural Adolescent Girls. New Delhi, Indraprastha Press.

Mathew, A., 1988. Importance of Recreation in Family Life. Paper Presented at Seminar on Home Science and Family Life Education, Institute of Home Economics, New Delhi.

Mathur, M.B., 1989. Adult Education and Social Change. Ambala Cantt, The Indian Publications, 143-211.

Mead, G.H., 1928. Cited by Lloyd, A.M. (1985) in Adolescence. New York, Harper and Row Publishers.

Merh, S., 1984. Inter Relationship Between Population Education and Family Life Education. The Journal of Family Welfare, 30(3), 3-18.

Meyers, K.M., 1993. Child Care in JOBS Employment and Training Programme, What Difference Does Quality Make?. Journal of Marriage and the Family, 55, 767-83.

Mohanty, J., 1991. Adult and Non-formal Education. New Delhi, Deep and Deep Publications.

Mohanty, S.B., 1988. Life Long and Adult Education. New Delhi, Ashish Publishing House.

Mushi, K.P, 1991. Participation of Adult Learners in Determining Training Needs; Some Observations from Tanzania. Perspectives in Education, 7(2), 89-95.

National Institute of Adult Education, 1992. Annual Plan

National Institute of Educational Planning and Administration, 1989. A Report on Non-formal Education Programme.

National Institute of Educational Planning and Administration, 1990. Hand Outs on Projectisation of Non-formal Education.

Nimbalkar, M.R., 1987. Adult Education and its Evaluation System. Delhi, Mittal Publications.

Norton, A.J., 1983. Family Life Cycle. Journal of Marriage and the Family, 45, 267-75.

NFE news letter, 1989. Andhra Pradesh, 3(3-4).

Oppenheimer, V.K., 1982. Work and the Family Life. New York, Academic Press, 14-87.

Pal, M. and Mathur, S.S., 1989. Socio-Economic Factors in Mate Selection. Indian Journal of Applied Psychology, 27 (2), 68-71.

Parekh, B.S., 1985. Population Education : Inception to Institutionalisation, New Delhi, NCERT.

Park, J.E., 1972. Cited by Rao, P.M. (1988) in Adolescence—A Perspective and a Need for Family Life Education, The Journal of Family Welfare, 35(2) : 42-47.

Parmar, S.B.S., 1987. The Rural Hindu Family in Continuity and Change. Allahabad, Vohra Publishers, 47-104.

Pati, S., 1989. Adult Education. New Delhi, Ashish Publishing House, 91-93.

Pilling, D. and Pringle, K.M., 1978. Controversial Issues in Child Development. London, Elek.

Pillai, S.K., 1990. Non-formal Education in India. New Delhi, Criterion Publications.

Rajkumari, 1985. Attitude of Girls Towards Marriage and a Planned Family. The Journal of Family Welfare, 31(3), 53-60.

Rao, S. and Patel, B.C., 1992. Who Decides Family Size. Social Welfare, 39, 4-5.

Rao, B.S.V., 1988. National Adult Education Programme in Visakhapatnam District. Delhi, Himalaya Publishing House.

Rao, V.V.P. and Rao, V.N., 1982. Marriage, the Family and Women in India, New Delhi: Heritage Publishers.

Ramalingeswaram, P., 1986. Accessability of Women to Health and Family Planning and Educational Services. Social Change (June-September), 97-99.

Ramabrahmam, I., 1988. Adult Education Policy and Performance. Delhi, Gian Publishing House.

Ramu, G.N., 1988. Family Structure and Fertility—Engineering Patterns in an Indian City. New Delhi, Sage Publication, 42-84.

Reddy, P.A., 1992. Determinants of Adult Education—Instructor Effectiveness. New Delhi, Uppal Publishing House, 33, 63-65.

Research Centre for Women Studies, 1990-91. Designing Family Researches : A Model, Contribution to Women Studies Series : 10, Bombay, SNDT Women University. 21-25.

Roy, P., 1973. Monitoring and Evaluating a Non-Formal Education Project for Rural Women in Andhra Pradesh. CSP, 10.

Roestam, K.S., 1992. Health and Population Education in Posyandu and PKK in Indonesia. IASSI, Quarterly, 2(2), 112-15.

Roosa, M.W., Tein, J.Y., Groppenbacher, N., Michaels, M. and Dumka, L., 1993. Mothers Parenting Behaviour and Child Mental Health in Families with a Problem Drinking Parent. Journal of Marriage and the Family, 55, 107-18.

Rodda, A., 1980. Women and the Environment. London, Zeal Books Ltd., 46-69.

Sahay, 1969. Cited by Goode, W.J. (1987) in The Family (2nd Ed.), New Delhi, Prentice Hall of India Pvt. Ltd.

Salkind, N.J. and Ambron, S.R., 1987. Child Development (5th edn.). Holt Rinehart and Winston Inc. New York.

Saraswathi, L.S., Seshan, V., Dighe, A. and Natpracha, P., 1989. Trainers Manual—Towards Shared Learning. Madras.

Saraswathy, T.S. (Ed.), 1982. Human Development, Marriage and Family Relations. Vol. 1, Baroda, M.S. University.

Sathe, A.G., 1987. Issues and Problems in Introducing Family Life Education for Boys and Girls of Secondary Schools. The Journal of Family Welfare, 56-67.

Sathe, A.G. and Sathe, S., 1984. Family Life and Sex Education Programmes for Late Adolescents and Young Adults. The Journal of Family Welfare, 31(1): 14-20.

Saylar, G.J., Alexander, M.W. and Lewis, J.A., 1981. Curriculum Planning for Better Teaching and Learning (4th ed.). New York, Holt, Rinehart and Winston.

Scanzoni, J., 1970. Opportunity and the Family. New York, Free Press.

Schvaneveldt, J.D., 1966. The International Frame Work in the Study of the Family, in Nye, F.I and Berardo, F. (Ed.) Emerging Conceptual Frame Works in Family Analysis. New York, Macmillan, 79-129.

Sharma, M., 1980. Planning and Evaluating Non-Formal Education, A Systems Model. Ambala, The Indian Publications, 9-33.

Sharma, P., 1988. Rural Women in Education—A Study in Under Achievement. New Delhi, Sterling Publishers Pvt. Ltd.

Sigmund, J., 1920. Cited by Lloyd, A.M. (1985) in Adolescence. New York, Harper and Row Publishers.

Simons, R.L., Beaman, J., Longer, R.D. and Chao, W., 1993. Stress, Support and Antisocial Behaviour Trait as Determinants of Emotional Well-being and Parenting Practices Among Single Mothers. Journal of Marriage and the Family, 55 (May), 385-98.

Singh, R.P., 1987. Non-formal Education an Alternative Approach. New Delhi, Sterling Publishers Pvt. Ltd.

South, S.J., 1991. Socio-economic Differentials in Mate Selection Preferences. Journal of Marriage and the Family, 53, 928-40.

Smith, W.M. Jr., 1970. Position Paper on Family Life Education. The Family Coordinator, 19(2).

Sullivan, H.S., 1953. Cited by Lloyd, A.M. (1985) in Adolescence. New York, Harper and Row Publishers.

Trivedi, B.K., Sandell, J. and Mathur, J.S., 1976. Sex Education and the National Family Planning Programme. Journal of Family Welfare, 23:62.

Tein, J.Y., Roosa, W.M. and Michaels, M., 1994. Agreement Between Parent and Child; Reports on Parental Behaviours. Journal of Marriage and the Family, 56, 341-55.

Thakur, D.C., 1988. Adult Education and Mass Literacy. New Delhi, Deep and Deep Publications.

UNESCO, 1988. Family Life Education (Package one). Bangkok, UNFPA.

UNICEF, 1988. The State of World's Children. A Summary.

Vlassoff, C., 1980. Unmarried Adolescent Females in Rural India; A Study of the Social Impact of Education. Journal of Marriage and the Family, 42(2), 427-36.

Zimmerman, S.L., 1989. Understanding Family Policy: Theoretical Approaches. London, Sage Publications.

Appendix

A Manual on Family Life Education

Introduction

The family as a basic unit of society, provides, the basic needs, educates, and works towards the harmonious growth and fulfilment of its members. The families of today are experiencing a tremendous influence of the social changes taking place due to urbanization, industrialization, technological advances, and other associated phenomena. They are caught in a process of change, which result in the restructuring of relationships, or in the redefinition of norms. Some of these notable changes have been occurring in familial, familial role performances, child rearing practices, and in socializing patterns. A lot of effort needs to be made by the families to adjust and to adapt to new changes considering the changing facets of modern families. Though the education for family living and the preparation for various life tasks and developmental needs begin in the family, there is a dire need to supplement this education through a carefully framed system of Family Life Education (FLE), for children and their family members.

FLE as a formally structured intervention to help members of the family has been practised for over a few decades. Yet even today, what FLE is and what FLE ought to be, remains the subject of a continuing debate. It is, however, accepted that the FLE approach is both preventive and developmental, and is directed

"To teach" people to "Live together", creatively and with affection in the family with respect to the theoretical under pinnings of the FLE, there is no fully accepted single frame of reference. Hence any frame considered should be viewed as open and liable to additions and modifications.

Sporadic efforts have already been made to introduce FLE in the formal schools notably by Family Planning Association of India. But noteworthy efforts were not made in the non-formal sector. The investigator made an attempt to introduce FLE in the non-formal education sphere for the following reasons :

- Non-formal adult education programme, as a nationwide activity intends to cover adolescents and adults.
- NFAEP stresses the values of co-operation, equality and group solidarity.
- NFAEP also aims at promoting the quality of family life.
- NFAEP serves as a channel to reach unreached young generation so as to strengthen their family lives.

Through a systematic research programme, the content for FLE was identified. A learner/expert oriented curriculum was developed in the form of a 'Manual', based on the FLE needs of Adolescent girl participants of NFAEP (Chittoor district). The manual was field tested and found to be beneficial to the unmarried adolescent girls. A well integrated programme of FLE could help families adopt themselves to new changes and assume greater responsibility for the transformation of society.

Conceptual Frame Work

Curriculum is a plan for providing sets of learning opportunities for persons to be educated. A FLE curriculum, in order to be relevant, must reflect the felt as well as the real needs of the target groups and also be within the frame work of national goals for Non-formal Adult Education Programme. Based on the findings of content analysis of NAEP primers (IPCL) and FLE needs of unmarried adolescent girl learners (as perceived by experts, married adult women and unmarried adolescent girls), a curriculum was drafted in the form of a manual to serve as a practical resource guide for animators/volunteers who are intended to be involved in teaching/training/communicating FLE. The existing animators manual (*Volunteerlaku Suchanalu*) of NAEP of Chittoor district was taken as a model for developing FLE curriculum, as the animators/volunteers were already oriented in the use of such manuals.

The curriculum consists of Introduction, Conceptual Frame work, Illustrations, Lessons and Evaluation Schedules. The conceptual frame work divides the FLE content into seven units.

1. Family
2. Family Roles and Responsibilities
3. Family Life Cycle
4. Family Needs and Resources
5. Marriage
6. Responsible Parent Hood
7. Family Welfare Services

Under these seven units all the sixteen (identified) topics were grouped. The lessons were planned for the topics deriving the information from various resource materials—manuals, handbooks, reports and other forms of curriculum materials that have been prepared in India, Malaysia, Philippines and Some Western countries for use in their respective FLE Programmes. For every lesson relevant illustrations were designed and an evaluation sheet consisting of ten questions and a scoring key was also developed. For each lesson the following learning activities were developed and presented under six dimensions.

1. Showing the picture the animator should raise the following questions

Relevant questions pertaining to the illustrations were framed to gather already known information (about the topic) from the participants. This helps the participants to identify the characters/ situations given in the picture and to recall their past experiences related to the picture.

2. Description of Picture

The situations illustrated in the picture were described under this dimension, to ensure proper understanding of the picture.

3. Things to be given thought

Under this, few thought provoking questions relevant to the topic were given, to initiate thinking and better participation.

4. Information

The conceptual and theoretical issues relevant to the topic were presented meaningfully.

5. Suggested activity

To reinforce the information imparted and to promote better understanding an activity was suggested, which is to be monitored by the animator involving all the participants.

6. FLEP evaluation schedule

To assess the FLE programme, a set of structured questionnaires consisting of 160 questions (i.e., 10 questions on each topic) and scoring keys were framed.

Unit I : Family

1. Concept of Family

Showing the picture, the Animator should raise the following questions

- Have you seen this picture ?
- What is it called ?
- Who are they ?

Description of picture

This is a family. The family has father, mother, a daughter and a son. The children are studying. The mother is supervising the children and mending a garment. Father is reading a news paper.

Things to be given thought

- What is the composition of your family ?
- Has every individual in your village a family ?
- What are the types of families existing in your village ?
- What are the characteristics of a nuclear family ?

- What are the characteristics of a joint family ?
- What are the characteristics of an extended family ?

Information

The Family is the only social institution other than religion that is formally developed in all societies, a specific agency incharge of a great variety of social behaviour and activities. The family is made up of individuals, but it is also a social unit, and part of a larger social network. Families are not isolated, self-enclosed social systems. It is within the family that the child is first socialised to serve the needs of a society, and not only its own needs.

Definition : The family is a basic unit of a society. The strength or weakness of any society is directly related to that of the family. The family refers to a group of individuals who are related by blood, marriage or adoption. The family is also a link between the past and the future. Because of this, having children is a very important issue among young married couples.

Types of families and their characteristics

a. Nuclear

1. Smallest and most elementary type of family
2. Composed of husband, wife and off spring
3. Basic unit of society
4. Self-supportive
5. Independent
6. Feelings are very intense
7. More privacy

b. Extended families

1. Composed of a husband, wife, off spring and others
2. Able to provide supportive services
3. Less privacy
4. Feelings are less intense

c. Joint families

1. Largest and oldest type of family
2. Composed of members of three generations related by blood/marriage

3. Self-supportive
4. Less strong conjugal relationships
5. Less privacy

Suggested activity

Group discussion on importance of family and concepts related to family may be initiated to promote better understanding.

2. Family Functions

Showing the picture, the questions to be raised by the animator

- What does the picture explain ?
- Did you ever come across the situation illustrated in the picture in your daily life ?
- Name the family function, illustrated in each sector ?

Description of picture

The picture depicts functions of a family. Each function is illustrated in each sector. Thus seven functions are illustrated.

Picture-1 : In this procreation function is illustrated. A mother is lying on a bed with a new born next to her. Father is standing next to the mother overlooking the mother and the new born.

Picture-2 : Father, mother, daughter and son are having a meal.

Picture-3 : Children (a girl and a boy) are going to school, mother is going through a book, father is reading a news paper.

Picture-4 : Mother and father are nursing a sick child.

Picture-5 : Mother, father, daughter and son are playing caroms.

Picture-6 : Father and daughter are attending to gardening work, mother and son are fetching water.

Things to the given thought

- From where does the citizens of a nation come from ?
- Where does the individuals learn basic behaviour ?
- It is whose responsibility to fulfil the basic needs of family members ?
- What is the result of failure of a family in performance of its functions ?

- What are the present functions of a family for future social change ?

Information

The family is the basic unit of a society. The strength and solidarity of a society is highly dependent on how this basic unit performs its functions. It is the responsibility of all members of a family to fulfil the family functions. However, the parents generally shoulder a large portion of it. Failure on the part of parents to perform their duties (thus not fulfilling family functions) can lead to social problems for many generations to come, e.g., parents. Who do not love their children will have children who do not know how to love; this will mean that they will not love their children in return. Social problems among our children can be traced back to failure of parents/families to perform their functions. The family serves society through :

1. Reproduction

The survival of a nation depends on the ability of couples to reproduce.

2. Physical maintenance

Basic needs of members have to be provided, if the family is to function properly. Basic needs include food, shelter, clothing. When members are too young to meet such needs themselves, it is the responsibility of parents to provide them. It is important that these needs be met adequately. A child without proper food will not grow up into a healthy person. A child without love perpetuates hate, etc.

3. Social placement for the child

At the time of birth the family provides us with an ascribed status, e.g., caste, race, physical build, etc. As we grow, the families help us find an "achieved" status, often one that is higher in the eyes of the society.

4. Socialisation and Social Control

A child born to a family is taught from the moment of birth, behaviour that is acceptable to the society.

5. Preparation of individuals for future social changes

Discrimination on the basis of sex, labelling the familial activities as feminine and masculine should be eliminated as women around the world are entering all spheres of work, there is no more gender bias within the family activities. This is done through examples or through teaching. The role behaviour learned from the family becomes the model for role behaviour in our society. This way, culture is passed down from generation to generation. Social control needs to be enforced from a very young age. Failure on the part of families to perform this can lead to distant behaviour, a problem to our society. The family maintains itself as an ongoing unit through :

- *Affection* : Affection is a product of family living. The family remains united through love.
- *Personal security and acceptance* : The family is the home base which we know we are part of it. It is a place for help and we know we will always be accepted. In a way it is the main source of mental and emotional health for its members.
- *Satisfaction and a sense of purpose* : The family provides us with a sense of satisfaction for efforts which may go unnoticed for the society. This is important for the mental health of an individual.
- *Continuity of Companionship and Association* : While we move from job to job and from town to town, friends and acquaintances are forgotten, but the family provides continuing companionship to all members. Companionship means a place to vent our troubles and a place to share our disappointments over many years.
- *Establishing limits* : Establishing limits and reinforcing a sense of what is right are two important functions of the family.

Suggested Activity

Gathering information from the participants about their family functions. Classification of family functions and assessing the performance of families and then finding solutions for better performance.

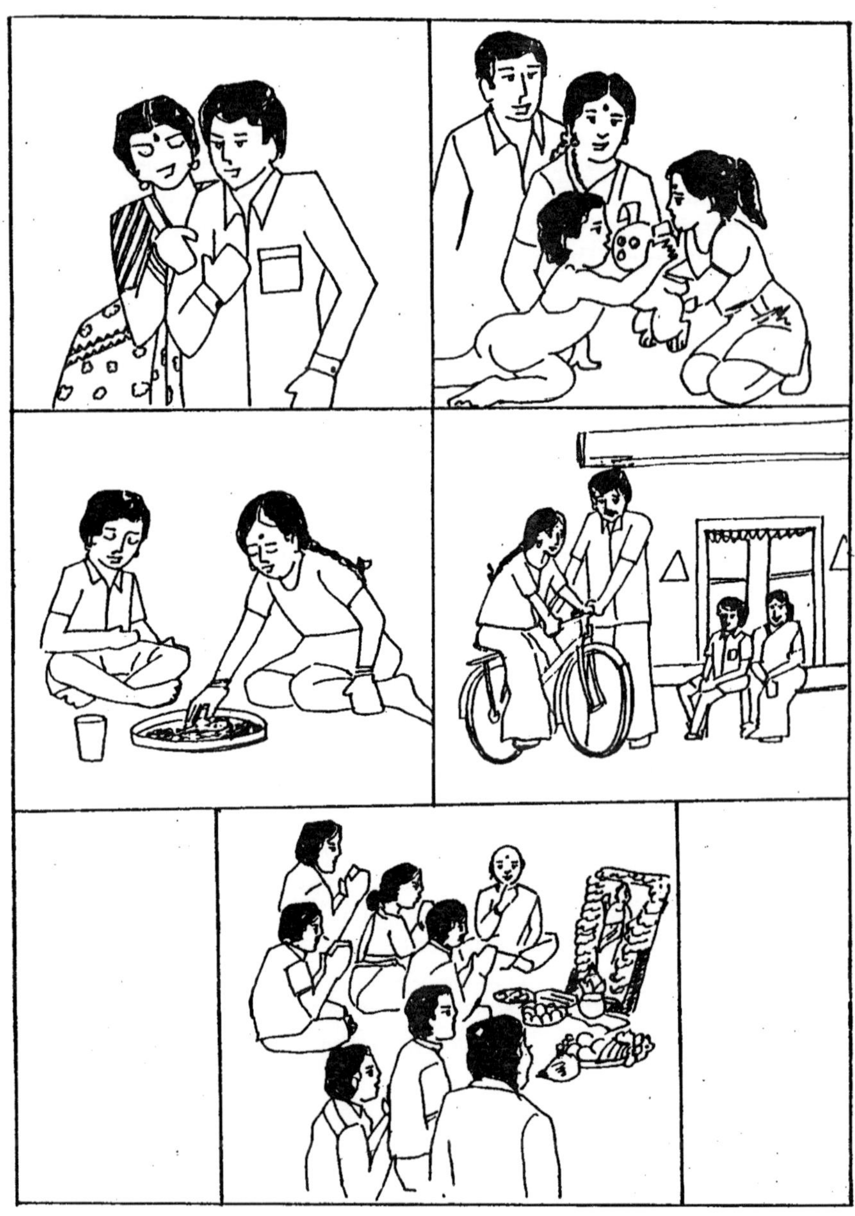

Unit II : Roles and Responsibilities

3. Family Roles and Relationships

Showing the picture,,the Animator should raise the following questions

- What do you see in this picture ?
- What are they doing ?
- Are the pictures in all the sections interrelated ?

Description of picture

The picture in all the sectors are interrelated

Picture 1 : Shows the picture of a newly married couple. They are husband and wife, they are a family.

Picture 2 : The couple have children (i.e., they have become parents) and they are taking care of their children.

Picture 3 : Sister is helping the brother in taking food. She is assuming the role of her parents in their absence and taking care of her brother.

Picture 4 : Father is teaching cycling to the daughter. Mother and son are watching. Daughter or son, children need to learn cycling irrespective of their sex.

Picture 5 : The family performs a function by inviting relatives and friends. The family maintains relationships with the members of the society.

Things to be given thought

- Does the roles of same individuals change during different stages of life ?
- Is knowledge about different familial roles necessary ?
- Is it necessary to maintain a healthy relationship among different roles ?
- What affects the relationships among family members ?
- What is the result of failure of members in their role performance ?

Information

Happiness and prosperity would prevail if everyone would behave "Correctly" as a family member. This meant primarily that no one should fail in his filial obligations. Family duties are the direct role responsibility of every one in the society, with rare exceptions. Moreover, many family role responsibilities cannot usually be delegated to others. A role refers to an expected behaviour in any social interaction. A clear understanding of roles is very important in the family. His interpretation or lack of understanding leads to problems and sometimes crises. The issue of roles with in the family is further complicated by change in the family system, i.e., change from joint to extended/nuclear families, participation of women in economic activities outside the home, influence of western culture and religion, etc.

The following can be said about family roles :

a Role definitions and boundaries are more likely to be sharply defined in large families than in small families.

b The marital role or the role of man and woman as couples provides for companionship, security, physical relationships, reproduction and friendship.

c As family size increases, parental role tend to become more important than marital role.

d Parents are basically responsible for the guidance and rearing of children, but the extended family and other members of the community may share this responsibility at different levels.

e Older children are often delegated parental responsibilities in large families.

f Parental roles are fulfilled more successfully if parents have basic knowledge of the factors that contribute to the growth and development of children.

g Parents also perform work roles to support and care of their families.

h The financial demands of large family can force parents to spend time on the work role to support the family.

i Roles played by family members and the time needed to be spent in each role differs with the stage of the life cycle and is very much influenced by cultural values. Family relationships can be affected by

- Communication.
- Conflicting expectation

- Personality
- Culture
- Needs of individuals.

Suggested activity

Ask the participants to recollect the roles within their families and present the same. Identify positive and negative aspects and initiate discussion to find solutions for the problems identified.

4. Family Responsibilities

Showing the Picture, the question to be raised by the animator

- What different activities do you see in the picture ?
- What do they indicate ?
- Are the pictures in all the pictures related ?

Description of the pictures

The pictures depict the responsibilities of a family, viz., provision of food, clothing, shelter, education, love and affection.
Picture 1 : The family is providing food to all the members.
Picture 2 : The family is providing clothing to all the members.
Picture 3 : The family members share love and affection. They have a sense of belongingness among themselves.
Picture 4 : The family provides shelter in the form of a home.
Picture 5 : The children are going to the school.

Things to be given thought

- What are the family responsibilities ?
- Can familial responsibilities be delegated to others ?
- Is fulfilment of basic needs a family's responsibility ?
- Know how, do how of each role responsibility should be learnt ?
- Does deprivation of basic needs lead to bigger social problems ?

Information

Responsibilities are the tasks to be undertaken by the members of

the family for the well being and maintenance of the family. Family duties are the direct role responsibility of everyone in the society with rare exceptions. Moreover many family responsibilities cannot usually be delegated to others. While in work situation specialized obligations can be delegated. Happiness and prosperity would prevail if everyone would behave "Correctly" as a family member. This meant primarily that no one should fail in his familial obligations. Satisfying the needs, viz., Food, Clothing, Shelter, Health, Education of family members is the responsibility of the family. Deprivation of these needs may lead to psycho-social problems, which in turn may weaken the family system and then the society.

It is necessary to create an awareness among the members of the family from a very early age about the expected role responsibilities and the necessary know-how and do-how needs to be imparted by the parents. It is also the responsibility of the family members to maintain family equilibrium within the family. The family is vulnerable to disequilibrium not only because of changes internally induced by members and its own developmental processes but because of inputs from the external environment as well. The family in its effort to maintain a homeostasis may not always serve the best interests of all its members. Yet it is the responsibility of the family members to safeguard the stability of the family.

Suggested activity

Based on the information transmitted ask the participants to examine their own family life and identify the responsibilities and share with the group.

Unit III : Family Life Cycle

5. Family Life Cycle

Showing the picture, the animator should raise the following questions

- What common things do you find in all these pictures ?
- What changes have you noticed in the pictures ?
- What do you understand from the pictures ?

Description of picture

There are 6 pictures

Picture 1 : A newly married couple, who constitute a family.
Picture 2 : The couple with a new born child, i.e., they are expanding their family through procreation.
Picture 3 : The couple with two children.
Picture 4 : The children are going to school, i.e., schooling stage.
Picture 5 : The children are grown up and become adolescents, i.e., launching stage.
Picture 6 : The old couple with newly married couples, i.e., son and daughter in-law, daughter and son-in-law (retiring stage)

Things to be given thought

- At what period of life does the founding stage start ?
- What problems do the couples encounter in expanding stage ?
- What is expected of the parents during the schooling stage ?
- At what age should the children be launched ?
- Besides these, are there any other stages in family life.

Information

Family life starts at the time of marriage and ends with the death of the couple. During this term, every family goes through five different stages of family life, namely :

- Founding stage,
- Expanding stage,
- Schooling stage,
- Launching stage,
- Retirement stage.

Founding stage

This stage covers the period from marriage to the birth of the first child. This is a stage of adjustment. The couple coming from different family setups start living together either alone or with the family of the bridegroom. Planning for future starts at this stage.

Expanding stage

This is the stage of expansion of individual family units. The birth of the children, and their rearing covers this stage. It frequently overlaps with other stages. It is a very important stage with regard to children. The parents' capabilities in care of children plays very important role. In our country where customs and practices are deep rooted, the young couple have to choose a right practice which is not offensive to the existing customs/practices especially when they are living with the parents. The demands on financial and physical sources of parents is also more.

The Schooling Stage

Schooling stage covers schooling years of children, viz., pre-primary, primary, high school, vocational school and university. Guiding, supervising and disciplining children are the major role responsibilities in this stage. The parents have to be understanding, patient, loving and suggest young one's in adjusting to the development.

Launching stage

The grown up children choose their vocation/employment and become earning members. The children marry and build their own families. The role of the parents in selection of life partners for children should be that of a counsellor/guide. The parents can help their young ones in choosing their life partner.

Retirement stage

The couple complete their familial responsibilities and continue to live with one or all the children or choose to live separately. The retired couple will have time to enjoy each others company. The responsibility of the old couple falls on the younger ones.

Suggested activity

Invite old couples to present their experiences during various stages of their life. Initiate discussion after the presentation and reinforce positive points.

Unit IV : Family Needs

6. Family Size

Showing the picture, the animator should raise the following questions

- How many members are there in the first picture ?
- How many members are there in the second picture ?
- What difference do you notice in the two pictures ?

Description of picture

Pictures of two families are presented. In picture 1, a small family consisting of a husband, wife and two children. The members are healthy and happy looking and in picture 2, a large family consisting of a husband, wife and four children. The members look dull, weak and unhappy.

Things to be given thought

- How many members are there in your family ?
- How many households are there in your village ?
- What is the population of your village ?
- What difference do you find in quality of life of small and large families ?

Information

The number of members in the family is called size of the family. There are small families and also large families. Small families will have a couple and less than three children. Large families will have a couple and more than three children. The bigger the size of the family the more number of members to share the family resources such as housing, food, money and materials. With the increase in size of a family, the income may not increase proportionately, which places more demands on existing resources which may not be sufficient to satisfy the physical needs of members. Which in turn reduces quality of life of the family and exerts more stress on the

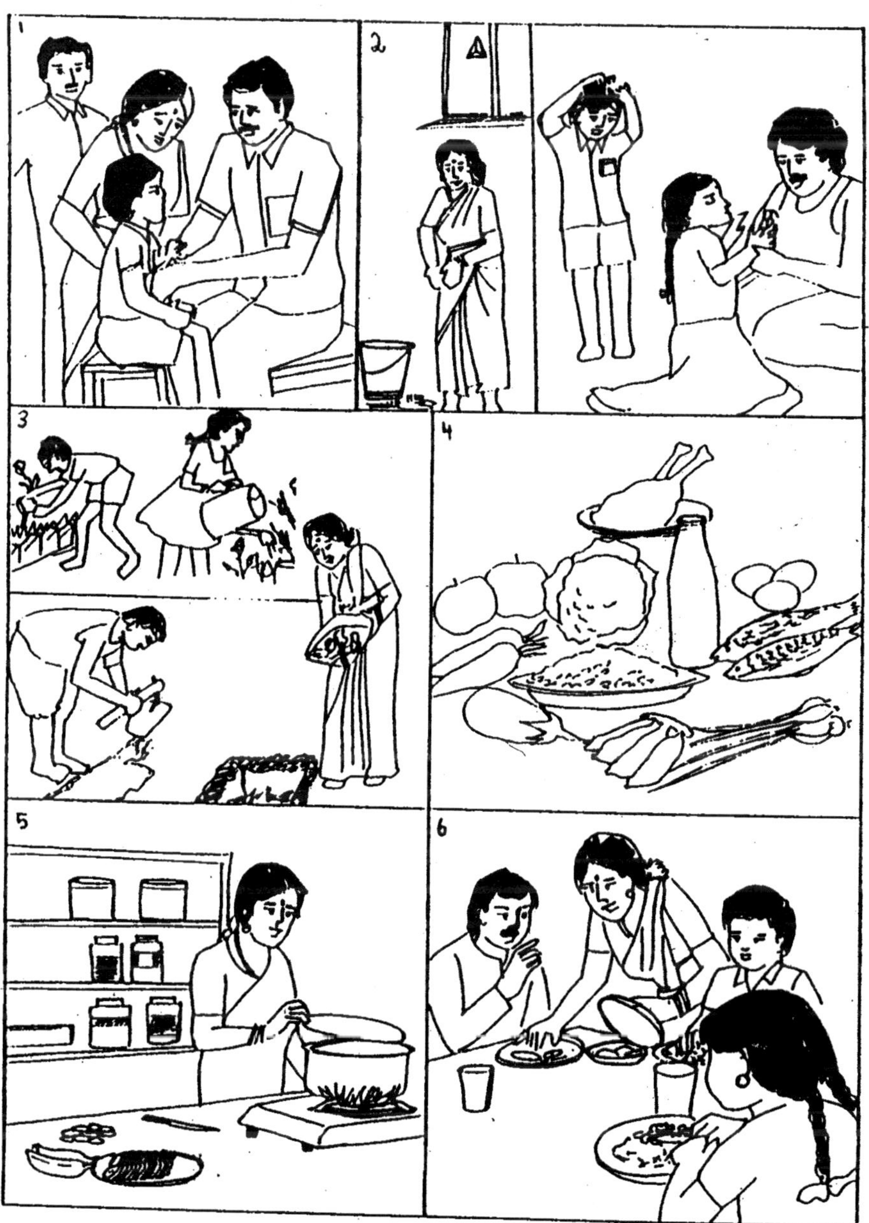
1
2
3
4
5
6

couple. The responsibilities of the couple will also increase. The life for which the children prepared may not be good. The children may be deprived of many physical needs, which leads to other psycho-social problems. Whereas the small families reduce :

- demands on family resources;
- better attention to the childrens' needs;
- responsibilities are reduced;
- maintenance of better family relations is possible;
- can lead to better quality of life.

Suggested activity

Calculate the expenditure per head in your own family, calculate the expenditure for the whole family. Assess the quality of life in your own family and relate it to your family size.

7. Health and Nutritional Needs of Family

Showing the picture, the animator should raise the following questions

- What activities do you see in these pictures ?
- Have you observed those activities in your day to day life ?
- What does each picture explain ?

Description of picture

There are six pictures presented in an order. They explain Health and Nutritional practices.

Picture 1 : The parents are getting their child immunized

Picture 2 : Father is cutting the nails of the daughter, while mother is washing her hands and feet in front of the house. The son is combing his hair. All the scenes in the picture explain about personal hygiene.

Picture 3 : Mother is dumping the waste in a composte pit, father is making a soakage pit and the children are tending to the garden. The picture depicts clean surroundings.

Picture 4 : Picture of Balanced diet

Picture 5 : Mother making a meal in covered vessels and cutting the vegetables in the right way.

Picture 6 : Male and female members of the family are sharing a meal equally irrespective of their sex.

Things to be given thought

- Are children in your family/in your neighbourhood immunized ?
- How good is your personal hygiene ?
- Does your family have clean surroundings ?
- Do you take a balanced diet ?
- Is sex discrimination shown in food distribution in your family ?

Information

Health and nutrition are interrelated. We eat food to satisfy hunger, But food does more than satisfying hunger. It performs three major functions. It gives us energy, supports our growth and development and provides resistance to common infections and diseases. The better and more nutritious is your food the more stronger and active you will be. Certainly you are what you eat. So our means should contain energy giving foods, body building foods and protective foods to perform various functions of the body effectively. Cereals and millets, fats and oils, sugar and jaggery are energy giving foods. Pulses, milk, meat, fish, egg, poultry and game are body building foods. Fruits and vegetable are protective foods.

Children, pregnant and lactating women require special nourishment. Children below five years age should be given high priority, as the growth rate during this period is high and susceptibility to diseases are also high. The diets of these children should be qualitatively good. School going children and adolescents need special nutritional care as theirs' is also a growing period.

Suggested activity

Ask the participants to assess the Health and Nutritional Practices prevailing in their own families. Suggest measures to improve their Health and Nutritional Practices.

2

8. Psycho-Social Needs of Family

Showing the picture, the animator should raise the following questions

- What do you see in the picture ?
- What does the actions of mother and father mean ?
- What feelings do you observe in the children ?
- Have you experienced such feelings in your family life ?

Description of the picture

In this picture the mother is giving a kiss to her son, Daughter is showing the progress card to her father and father is holding the daughter close to him and patting her. In another scene, the father is talking to the teacher in the presence of children. The children and father look confident and happy.

Things to be given thought

- Does every individual have psycho-social needs ?
- Are these needs different at different stages of life ?
- What happens, when these needs are not fulfilled ?
- How can a family fulfil these needs of its members ?

Information

Every individual is unique. Besides physical needs every individual has psycho-social needs which are expected to be fulfilled by the family. Fulfilment of these needs shapes the individual into a happy one. Unfulfilment may lead to dissatisfaction and unhappiness. In extreme conditions, it may lead to behavioural problems, viz., emotional instability, quarrelsomeness, resentment of authority and restlessness.

The following are the psycho-social needs

Love

The child craves for affectionate relations with others. Children who receive genuine affection and know that adults truly care for them tend to see themselves as persons of worth and loveable. Children who are genuinely loved for themselves without any conditions attached develop, strong positive self-concepts and have little need to try to obtain love and attention from others in an immature and emotional manner.

Security

Children must feel safe and protected. They need to see the world as reliable, safe and non-threatening. Parental behaviour which is unjust and inconsistent appears to make the child feel anxious and that the world is unsafe and unreliable. The family should help the children to perceive themselves as having the inner resources to deal successfully with the world.

Acceptance

The family members should adopt an "I am O.K.—you are O.K." approach to human relationships. Children who are genuinely accepted develop a sense of belongingness and security. Children who are not accepted are likely to feel rejected and undersirable, such persons may not accept others also.

Trust

Trust is developed when ones physical and emotional needs are satisfied and perceive the world as good and reliable. If these needs are not satisfied, they are prone to develop mistrust and feel that the world is hostile and unreliable.

Self esteem

The children have strong needs to value themselves and their contributions. They need recognition, attention and appreciation to build their system. When needs for self esteem are not met they develop teaching of inferiority, inadequacy and helplessness.

Limits

The establishment of limits and boundaries to check the freedom of the children who have been free remains necessary. This is to help the child to be self directive and balance the behaviour sensibly.

Janata Fridge
POST-OFFICE
SAVINGS
DEPOSIT

Freedom

Children should be given freedom within reasonable limits to explore, to be independent, to make decision and learn. Lack of freedom makes the children to be dependent on their parents and peers.

Suggested activity

Ask the participants, whether their own psycho-social needs are satisfied and help them to find reasons for unfulfilment of these needs.

9. Management of Family Resources

Showing the picture, the animator should raise the following questions

- What do you see in these pictures ?
- What does each picture explain ?
- Have you come across such an activity in your own family ?

Description of picture

The pictures are presented in an order to explain about methods of managing family resources.

Picture 1 : The housewife is counting and allotting money for various activities.

Picture 2 : The housewife is making purchases while looking at a shopping list.

Picture 3 : The housewife is using labour saving devices such as Janata fridge, Haybox, Solar cooker and utilising the leisure time for constructive work.

Picture 4 : The housewife is depositing money saved in a post office.

Things to be given thought

- What is the total income and expenditure of your family ?
- What are the areas of waste ?
- How to cut down unnecessary expenditure ?
- What are the safe saving methods ?

- How to conserve family material resources ?
- How to save energy and time ?

Information

Management of family resources include planning, selection, purchasing, storage and utilisation of family resources. Maintenance of few records will help the family members in making better plans for future. Estimation of Total income both in cash and kind, and estimation of future needs are necessary for planning family budget. Many of us forget to plan for our future. It is observed that with the increase in income the percentage of income spent on food is reduced. In low income families major amount of income is spent on food. Food selection and purchase has to be done carefully. Buy what you need and what you can store only. Proper selection and storage of food avoids wastage and food spoilage. By deducting the food materials on hand from the food materials purchased one can get the total food consumed in a week/month. This calculation helps to decide how much food the family needs per a week/month. Calculate the cost of food needed per week/month and use VID model to control expenditure. List out the items to be purchased and assign V or I or D to each item, i.e., 'V' denotes vital, 'I' denotes important, 'D' denotes desired. Give priority to the items listed under 'V' if budget permits 'I' items can also be purchased, 'D' items can be purchased if surplus amount of money is available. This method of categorising the items, helps in reduction of waste by purchasing the items which are needed only.

Some points for better cost control

1. Plan your daily activities ahead of time
2. Planning daily activities saves time and energy
3. Purchase what you need and can store
4. Use of low cost labour saving devices saves, time and energy
5. Safe saving and investment methods assure security
6. Pre-preparation before cooking helps in conservation of fuel and time
7. Recycling of waste water conserves water.

Suggested activity

Ask the participants to calculate their family's total income and expenditure, also ask them to identify other material resources.

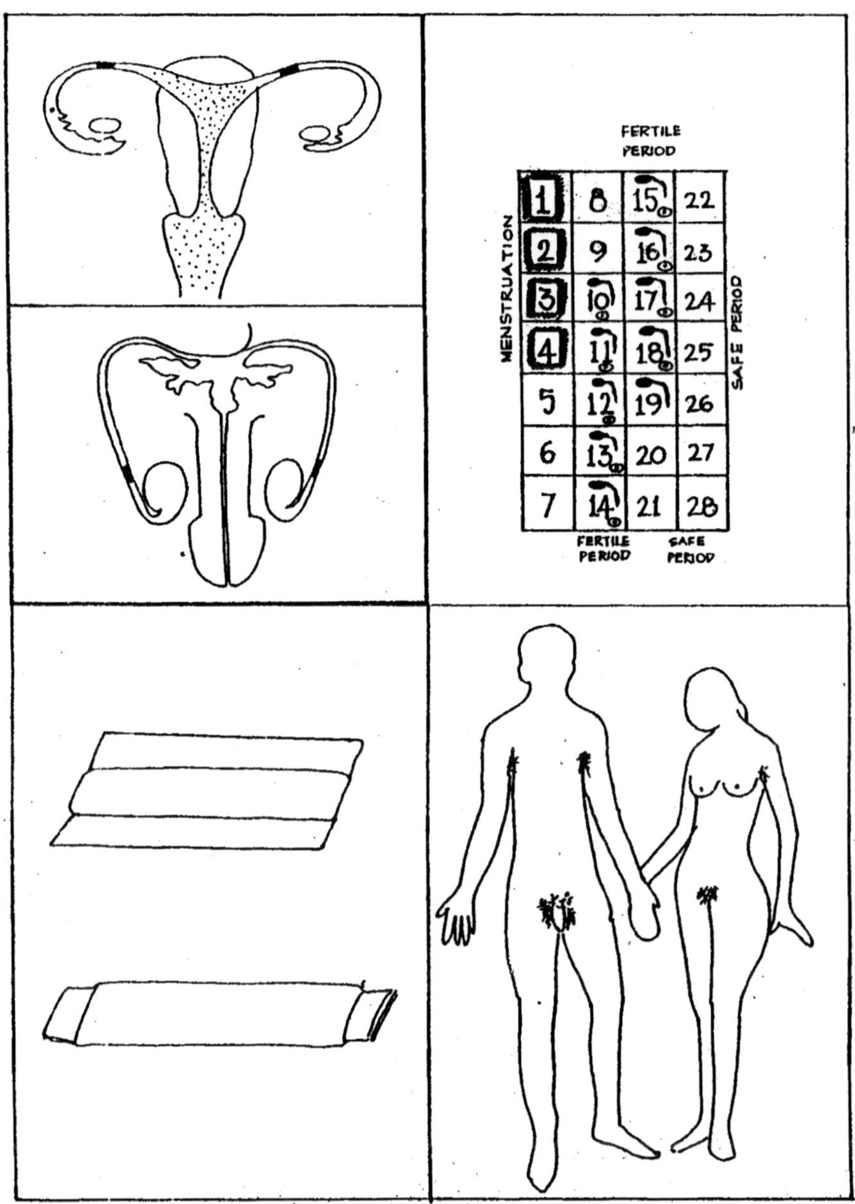
FERTILE
PERIOD
MENSTRUATION
1 8 15 22
2 9 16 23
3 10 17 24
4 11 18 25
5 12 19 26
6 13 20 27
7 14 21 28
SAFE PERIOD
FERTILE
PERIOD
SAFE
PERIOD

Ask them to assess the amount of time and energy spent on each activity. Initiate discussion to find solutions for the problems identified.

Unit V : Marriage and Family Life

10. Menstruation and Changes in the Body

Showing the picture, the animator should raise the following questions

- What do you see in these pictures ?
- Are you aware of the things shown in the picture ?
- What do they explain ?

Description of picture

A set of pictures arranged in an order explains about the female reproductive system, changes in the body, management during menstrual period.

Picture 1 : Female reproductive system consisting of ovaries, the uterus and tube.

Picture 2 : Shows the menstrual cycle and safe period.

Picture 3 : Shows the method of preparation of sanitary pads

Picture 4 : Shows the growth of secondary sex organs such as hair under armpits and around genital organs, development of breasts and hipbones.

Things to be given thought

- At what age does menstruation start ?
- What is menstruation ?
- What changes occur in the female body ?
- How to manage one-self during the period ?

Information

The monthly cycle in the girls is controlled by the glandular system. Menstruation is monthly bleeding in women which starts as early as eleven years of age to sixteen years. In most women menstruation occurs every 27 days for three days or so, although this may vary from one persons to another.

A woman's reproductive organs consist of ovaries, uterus or womb and tube that connects them. When the girl matures, the ovaries start producing an egg, every month. The egg, if not fertilised, comes into the uterus and inner cover of the uterus breaks off along with the egg and comes out of the body. This process is called menstruation. The ovaries start producing an egg two weeks (14 days) after the first day of menstruation which, if not fertilized results in menstruation. During normal menstruation a girl loses a relatively small amount of blood, usually less than half a cupful, and her body soon makes this up again. However, if bleeding is excessive and pain rather severe, medical attention has to be sought. For preparation of pads, clean cloth, with cotton can be used. If cloth is used, soiled cloth can be washed with a detergent and dried in a clean place under the sun and used again. Private parts (genitalia) should be cleaned regularly with water and the pads should be changed every day. Poor sanitation during menstrual period may cause diseases which may lead to childlessness.

Beginning of menstruation is the time when a girl grows most rapidly. Her breasts begin to develop and hair begin to grow under her armpits and around the genital organs. Hip bones take round shape, which is very important for the growth of the child when she gets pregnant and also for easy delivery. The womb also attain its full size at the age of 18. The growth of the reproductive organs of a girl is completed only when she is eighteen years old. If she gets pregnant before that the health of the girl and child gets affected. The girls can eat normally and attend to their daily activities during menstrual period.

Suggested Activity

Motivate participants to share their experiences and initiate discussion, clarify doubts.

11. Mate Selection

Showing the picture, the animator should raise the following questions

- Whom do you see in the picture ?

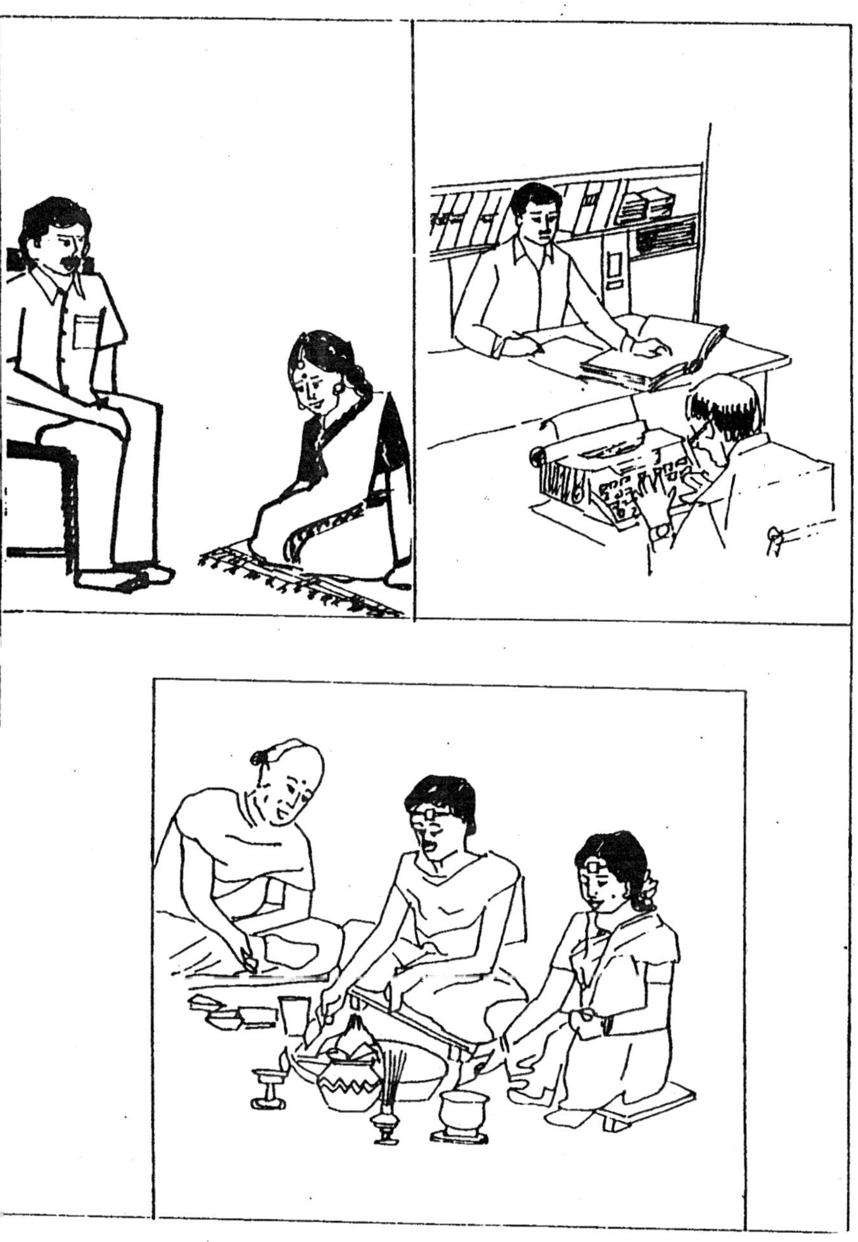

- What do you understand from them ?
- Have you come across such incidence ?

Description of picture

There are three pictures related to mate selection

Picture-1 : The picture shows a boy and a girl. The boy is older than the girl. The girl is physically matured. The picture is highlighting the age of the couple.

Picture-2 : The bridegroom looks matured, educated and has earning capacity. The picture shows the bridegroom receiving his wages from the employer, i.e., he is economically independent.

Picture-3 : The picture depicts the boy and girl to be married showing their consent non-verbally.

Things to be given thought

- What qualities are desired in a bridegroom ?
- What is the right age for marriage ?
- What are the consequences of wrong choice of a mate ?

Information

Every human society has some kind of mate selection procedure which functions to sort out males and females as marriage partners. In India, though rapid changes have occurred in ways of living, traditional cultural practices continue to co-exist, especially in marriage and family issues. It is the responsibility of the elder members of the family to choose a suitable bride or bridegroom for their children. In this context the person to be married has limited choice. Yet the girl's/boy's likes and dislikes are usually taken into consideration. Usually the bride or bridegroom's caste, family background, education, employment, physical appearance and socio-economic status are taken into consideration while selecting as a marriage partner. In some cases horoscope of the boy or girl is also considered.

The boys/girls who are entering into family life should have a practical outlook about their marriage partners. Boys/girls age, educational status, personality, level of economic independence should be given priority. Marriage is an important stage in one's life. A boy or a girl who enter into marital life are expected to live with the marital partner throughout their life. In this context the

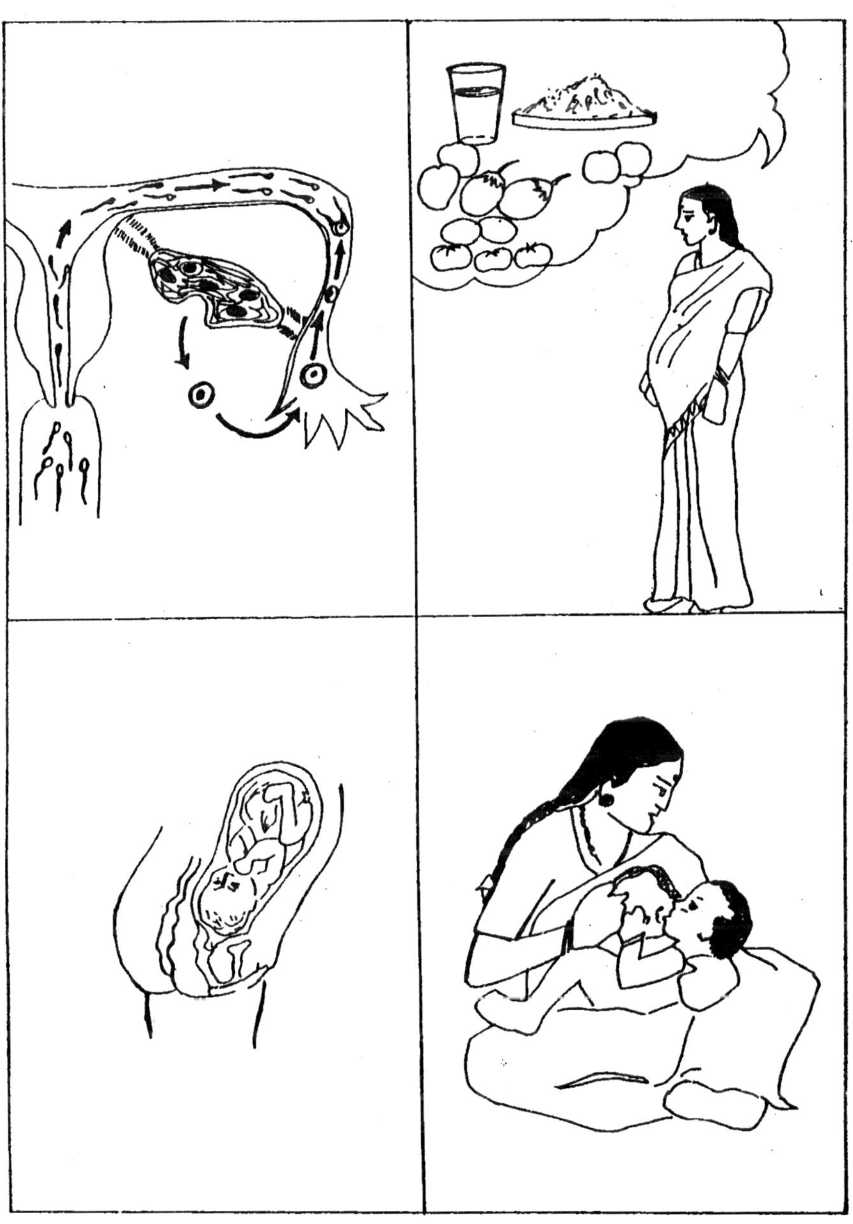

mate selection assumes greater importance. The choice of the mate should be made with the consent of the girl and the boy.

Suggested Activity

Invite two or three married couples to explain the problems they have encountered in selection of a mate and adjustmental problems. Initiate discussion on the topic and draw conclusions.

12. Pregnancy and Child Birth

Showing the picture, the animator should raise the following questions

- What do you see in these pictures ?
- What do you understand from these pictures ?
- Are they familiar to you ?

Description of picture

The pictures explain about conception, pregnancy and child birth.

Picture-1 : Shows the female reproductive system and union of egg with the sperm.

Picture-2 : Shows a pregnant woman with enlarged belly, taking a balanced diet consisting of rice, pulse, meat foods, milk, vegetables and fruits.

Picture-3 : Shows a growing foetus in the uterus.

Picture-4 : Shows a new born baby, breast fed by the mother.

Things to be given thought

- What is conception ?
- What changes occur in a woman's body during pregnancy ?
- What care should be taken during pregnancy ?
- What care should be taken during delivery ?
- What should be fed to the new born ?

Information

A girl/woman's reproductive organs consist of ovaries, which produce an egg, fourteen days after the first day of menstruation. The egg if fertilised leads to pregnancy which is called conception.

Menstruation stops after conception and sometimes the pregnant woman may feel like vomiting especially in the morning, which is called morning sickness. During pregnancy the belly of the woman grows bigger and breasts also become bigger and firmer. The foetus in the mother's womb continues to grow taking food from the mother's body. Hence the mother has to take food sufficient for the two people (i.e., the mother and the baby).

Mother needs good food (like milk, egg, meat, fish, cereals, vegetables and fruits, fats and oils) and rest. Pregnant women must undergo health checkup periodically and she has to be immunized against tetanus twice. Iron and calcium supplementation in the form of tablets or tonics can be taken on doctors advice to prevent deficiency problems. The pregnant woman should be admitted into a nearby PHC or hospital for the delivery. Otherwise a trained dai or health worker's help has to be taken. At the time of delivery the mother undergoes mild to severe birth pains. These pains may last for 8 to 24 hrs, especially if it is a first delivery. At the time of child birth, a thick fluid called amniatic fluid comes out of the birth canal followed by baby who usually comes out upside down. After a little while, the umbilical cord comes out, which is to be cut with a sterilised scissors and tied with a sterilized thread.

As soon as the baby is born, it will cry. The baby's mouth, nose should be cleaned to ensure normal breathing and then covered with a fresh cloth. The baby should be put to breast as soon as possible. The first milk 'colostrum' protects the baby against diseases and keeps the baby healthy. The baby's date and time of birth has to be registered and a birth certificate has to be obtained from the Births and Deaths registration office.

Suggested Activity

Invite a local dai to explain about local superstitions and her experiences and initiate discussion, to promote better understanding.

13. Family Planning

Showing the picture, the animator should raise the following questions

- What do these pictures explain ?
- Are they familiar to you ?

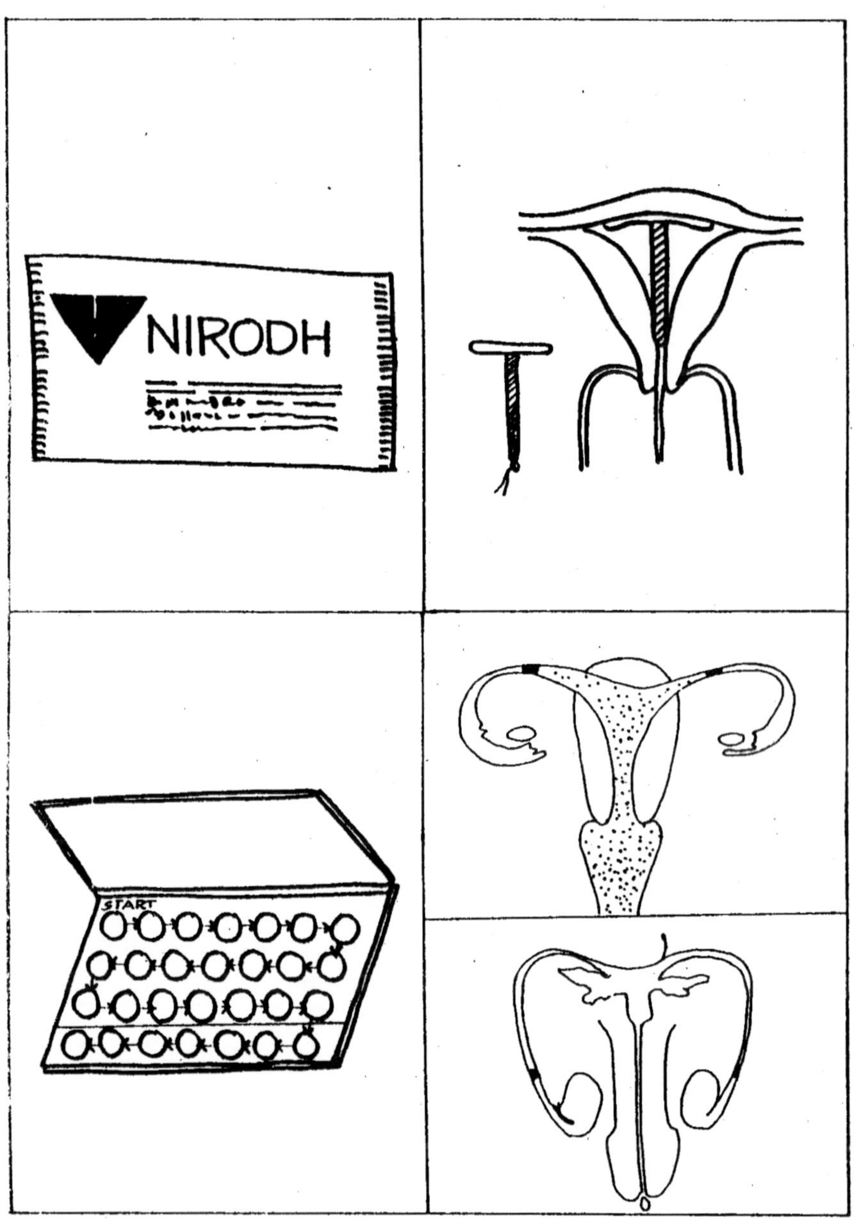
NIRODH
START

Description of picture

The picture shows family planning methods, viz., Nirodh, Oral contraceptives, Copper T, Tubectomy and Vasectomy.

Things to be given thought

- What are the benefits of family planning ?
- What are the different methods of family planning ?
- How to choose a right method of family planning ?

Information

Family planning is not only avoiding having children or having small families, but is also a way of promoting the welfare of the family by making every child wanted by protecting the health of mothers, children and the whole family.

Family Planning methods are used:

- by newly married couple to postpone the arrival of a child
- by new parents to postpone the arrival of a second child
- by poor parents to gain financial strength to support a child
- by a sick mother who required time to recover the strength and health to give birth
- by a couple, who have had many children and would like to stop having children.

Family Planning Methods

Family planning methods are two types one is to avoid pregnancy temporarily, other is to avoid having children permanently.

Temporary methods of family planning

Nirodh : This method is used by men. It prevents man's sperms (beej) from entering the womb. Therefore fertilization cannot occur.

Oral contraceptives

Pills : These are tablets, one tablet is to be taken every night by the woman starting on the fifth day after menstruation. The tablets prevent eggs from being produced every month, hence no pregnancy occurs.

Copper-T : It is a T-shaped wire, which is inserted in the womb. It prevents fertilization and pregnancy. This method may cause pain and excessive bleeding in the first few months. In such a case one must consult a gynaecologist.

Permanent methods of family planning

Tubectomy : It is a minor operation done to women. The tube that carries the egg is cut, so that the egg cannot move towards the womb to get fertilized and thereby prevents pregnancy.

Vasectomy : It is a minor operation done to men. The tube that carries the man's beej/sperms is cut, so that it cannot reach the egg to get fertilized and thereby prevents pregnancy.

Right methods of family planning should be chosen in consultation with a doctor or a health worker.

Suggested Activity

Arrange for demonstration of Family Planning tools and initiate discussion to clarify participants doubts.

Unit VI : Responsible Parent Hood

14. Care of Children

Showing the picture, the animator should raise the following questions

- What do you see in this picture ?
- What does the picture explain ?
- Are the activities shown in the picture familiar to you ?

Description of picture

The set of pictures explain about child care.

Picture-1 : Shows mother giving bath to the child

Picture-2 : Shows a child being immunized

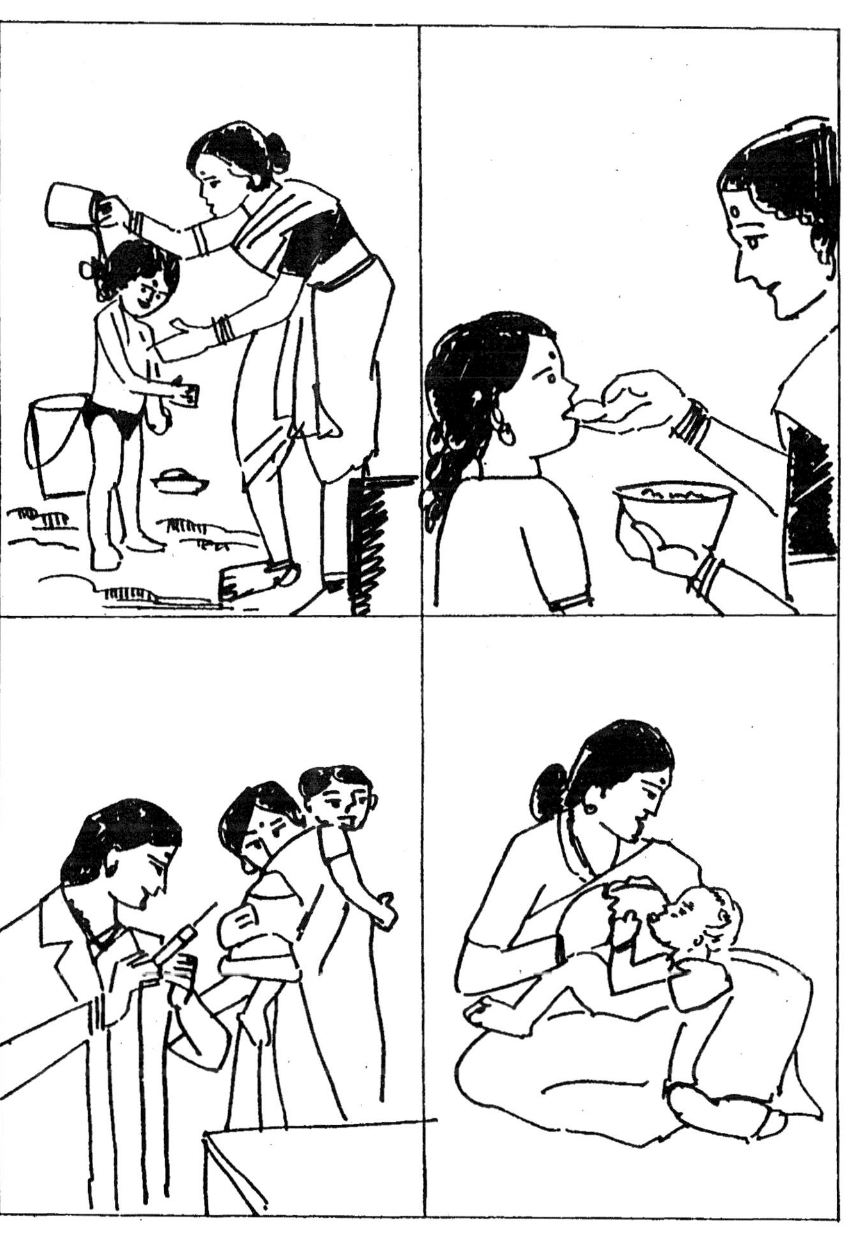

Picture-3 : Shows weaning foods to be given to the child
Picture-4 : Shows mother breastfeeding the child

Things to be given thought

- Till what age the child can be breast fed ?
- When to start giving other food ?
- How can a mother keep herself and the child clean ?
- How to prevent infections in children ?
- When to immunize the child ?

Information

A new born grows into a healthy child for which he requires care and nourishment. The new born should be protected from infections, which are mainly caused due to poor hygiene. Every mother should follow the following :

- The mother should keep herself and the child clean.
- The mother should clean her breasts before feeding. If bottle feeding is to be given, the bottles and the nipples have to be sterilized before every use.
- The child should be immunized regularly for which the local health worker is to be consulted. Immunization protects the child from communicable diseases.
- If the child is sick, she has to be taken to a health worker or a doctor. The child should not be taken to a local quack.
- The mother has to be vigilant and observe the child's development, especially in areas of speech, hearing, auditory and motor. In case of delayed development the child has to be taken to a nearby hospital.
- The mother should continue breast feeding, even after one year. But from the fourth month onwards, breast feeding is to be supplemented with other foods such as cereals, pulses, egg, meat, fish, vegetables and fruits. These supplementary foods should be well cooked, mashed, soft and easy to chew and digest. These foods have to be introduced one at a time.
- The mother/mother substitute should carefully guard the child in order to avoid any accidents.
- The toys chosen for children should be made with non-toxic material, it should not have sharp edges and should be easy to clean.
- The clothes chosen for children have to be comfortable, easy

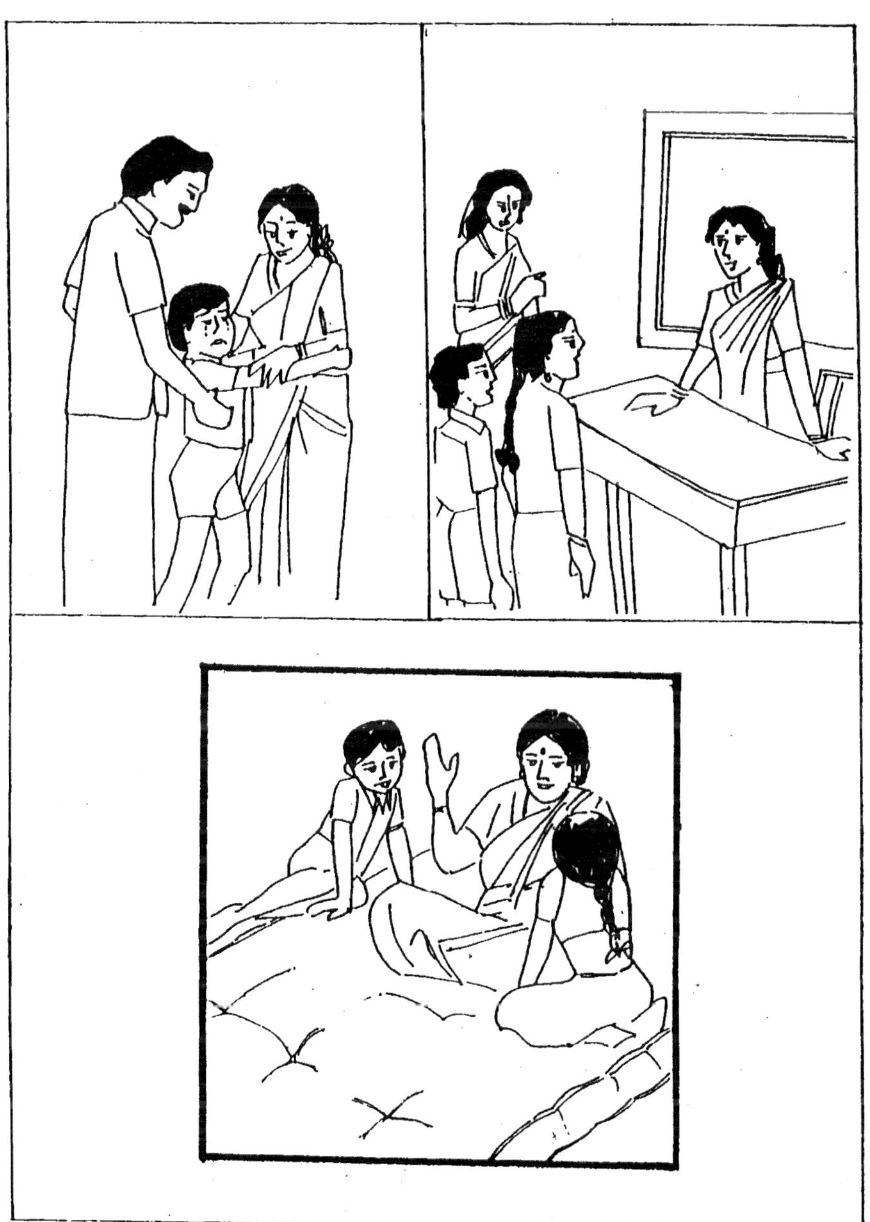

to put on and remove, easy to clean and maintain.
- Good care of infants and young children, avoids lot of health problems.

Suggested activity

Identification of problems in child care in the neighbourhood and discussion of the same.

15. Good Parenting Practices

Showing the picture, the animator should raise the following questions

- What do you see in this picture ?
- What does the picture explain ?
- Have you come across such a scene in your daily life

Description of picture

The picture shows family scenes; parents are consoling a crying child

Mother is discussing child's scholastic performance with the teacher.

Mother is listening to the child.

Things to be given thought

- How parents should behave with the children ?
- How to handle the child in difficult situations ?
- What is the effect of parents behaviour on child ?

Information

A child's personality depends upon his status in the family. Children who are deprived of parental attention may develop adjustment problems in the society. Usually parents tend to be more affectionate and protective towards the first child till the arrival of the second child. More often the last child is more pampered and given the things used by his elder siblings which may create a feeling of unhappiness in him. Many couples prefer small families having two children. The parents should not discriminate between the children-any kind of discrimination may lead to serious behavioural problems as they grow up. It is necessary that parents should be educated about these problems and advised to be consistent in their behaviour and should treat their children equally. Here are some do's and don'ts which the parent should follow

Don'ts

- Should not compare children with each other or others
- Do not refer anything without explaining the reason, for doing so
- Do not differentiate between/among the children
- Do not criticise the child
- Do not discuss about the child with others in front of him/her
- Do not force the child to do something beyond his/her capacity
- Do not abuse the child

Do's

- Allow the child to express his/her feeling freely
- Respect child's feelings
- Appreciate and encourage the child when he/she does something well
- Every day spend some time with the child
- Introspect your own behaviour
- Accept the child as he/she is
- Be confident and balanced in front of your children

As parents one must aim for a happy family.

Suggested activity

Introspection of ones own parents behaviour based on the information imparted in the session and realising the effect of the do's and don'ts (listed in the lesson) may help the participants in better understanding of the information.

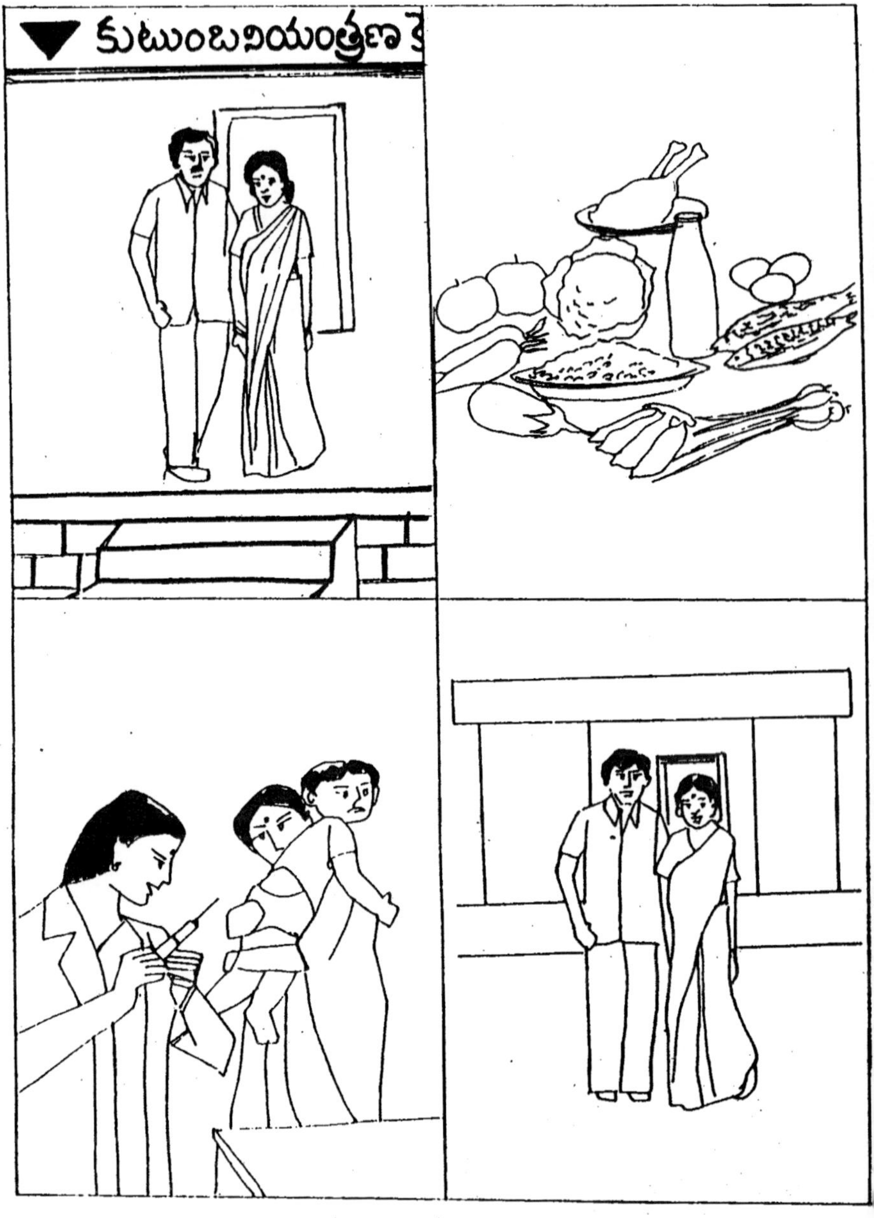

కుటుంబనియంత్రణ

Unit VII : Family Welfare Services

16. Family Welfare Services

Showing the picture, the animator should raise the following questions

- What do you see in the picture ?
- Do you have those services in your village ?
- Have any of your family members availed those services ?

Description of picture

The pictures relevant to the topic are presented, they are as under.

Picture-1 : Shows a pregnant woman getting supplementary food and education from an Anganwadi Centre.

Picture-2 : A new born child is being immunized

Picture-3 : A couple are being counselled in Family Counselling Centre.

Things to be given thought

- What are the family welfare services available in PHCs and at the village level
- Where are these service agencies located
- How and when to utilise these services
- What can we do to ensure that services are made available to us.

Information

The Government of India provides family welfare services to citizens through the departments of Medical and Health Services, Social Welfare, Women and Child Welfare and Human Resource Development. Under the department of Medical and Health Services for every 1,00,000 population a Primary Health Centre (PHC) is formed at the Mandal level. In every PHC, there will be a Doctor, Pharmacist, Nurses, Laboratory Technician, Health Inspector and Health workers. Besides these staff a Mandal

Extension Officer for Health will also be there at Mandal Level. A Health worker is in charge of 5,000 population. She/he makes home visits, identifies the health needs and offers health services such as Immunization, Pre and Postnatal care, Family Planning, Health Checkup, Treatment and Medication for various diseases. All these services are rendered free of cost.

Social welfare department through voluntary organisations extends daycare services for children and handles problem such as social evils. Women and child welfare department co-ordinates its programmes with that of Department of Medical and Health Services and attends to health problems of women and children. They also extend assistance to Balwadi and training of Balwadi personnel.

Department of Human Resource Development through ICDS programme provides Health and Nutrition Education to mother, Supplementary Nutrition to children, Pregnant and Lactating mothers, Pre-primary Education to children, Referral Services, Family Planning, etc., through Anganwadi centres. Anganwadi teachers and Ayahs undergo special training in extending the above mentioned services to beneficiaries. Anganwadi teachers also maintain good rapport with the beneficiaries and others. People need not be afraid of utilising the Family Welfare Services which are specially meant for them.

Suggested Activity

Organise a survey of Family Welfare Services available in your own area and initiate discussion in order to assess the quality and regularity of services.

Index

Acchpal, 41, 46
Adams, 26, 48
Adolescent girls, 65
Adult Education Centre, 34-35
  Impact on women, 35
Adult married women, 65
Aldous, 91
American Home Economics Association, 6, 39, 47
Anil, 34
Animator, 65
Audinarayana, 53
Avery, 40

Balu, 40, 45
Bedi, 18
Benedict, 22, 47
Boring, 28
Bowlby, 93
Buroes, 16

Central Advisory Board of Education, 28
Chandrasekar, 28
Chittoor dist., 52
Chittoor Zilla Saksharata Samithi, 52
Confucius, 9
Curriculum, 65, 124
Curriculum for National Adult Education, 35, 48

Dahama, 56
Dave, 41, 46
Davis, 53
Demographic profile of respondents, 66-75
  Age, 66-67
  Caste, 67-70
  Family income, 72-75
  Size of family, 70-72
  Type of family, 70
Department of Women and Child Development, 27
Desai, 11, 14-16, 19, 44, 70
Dhar, 41, 42, 46, 100
District Adult Education Board, 33
Dorrey, 57

Education Commission 1964-66, 28
Elder, 91
English and English, 65
Erikson, 22, 47
Eshleman, 10
Experts, 65
Exposure to FLE information 75-87, 118-20, 123-24

Depicted in Telugu Media, 83-84
Exposure to FLE through ACP, 79-81
Need for more information taught in AEP, 81-82
Need for publication and distribution in book form, 82
Number of cinema viewed, 84-85
Respondent's opportunities to know, 75-77
Satisfaction with information imparted in AEP, 81
Sources helpful in special efforts to acquire and practise, 79
Special efforts to acquire and practise, 78-79
Telecast in Doordarshan, 86-87
Through AIR broadcast, 83
Through film show, 86
Utilisation of, 77-78

FAO, 20
Family concept in population, 4
Family income and FLE need perception, 100-09, 121-22
Caste and, 100
Content analysis of NAEP primers of Chittoor dist., 102-07
FLE manual, 107-09
FLEP evaluation schedule, 109
Marital status and, 101-02
Type of family and, 100-01
Family life education for adolescent girls, 1-8, 113
Adolescence period of, 1
Aims of, 113
Conceived and implemented, 5
Conclusion, 123-24
Definition of, 2, 114
Education for family life, 1
Factors responsible for, 5
Hypothesis, 8, 116
Non formal adult education, 7, 14
Objectives of, 2-3, 7, 115-16
Planning and implementation, 6
Population and, 5-6
Population of adolescents, 1
Social welfare and family welfare centres, 2
FLE manual, 107-09, 122-23
Description of picture, 108
Information, 108
Showing picture the Animator, 108
Suggested activity, 109
Things to be given thought, 108
FLE programme impact on NAEP participants, 110-12, 122, 124
FLE knowledge of NAEP participants, 110-11
Impact of, 111-12
Family Planning Association of India, 2-3, 7, 42-43, 114
Population education programmes, 3-4
Restricted by time allotted to schools, 5
Family Welfare Programmes, 7
Freud, 22, 47
Friedlander, 10

Gandhi, Mahatma, 19, 29-30
Gangrade, 24-25
Garg, 24

Gesell, 22, 47
Gokan, 46
Gokarn, 36, 41, 114
Goldthorpe, 96
Goode, 10, 11
Gopalan, 1, 26, 49, 93
Gore, 15
Grihini Training Programmes, 5, 38, 47, 114

Hall, 22, 47
Harris, 93
Hill, 91

Identification of FLE needs, 87-98, 120-21
- Children care, 97
- Family functions, 89-90
- Family life cycle, 91-92
- Family planning methods, 96-97
- Family responsibilities, 90-91
- Family roles and relationship, 90
- Family size, 92
- Family Welfare Services, 98
- Good parenting practices, 97-98
- Health and nutrition needs, 92-93
- Management of family resources, 94
- Mate selection 95-96
- Menstruation and changes in body, 94-95
- Preference of experts, married adult women and unmarried adolescent girls for, 87-89
- Pregnancy and child birth, 96
- Psycho-social needs of family 93

Integrated Child Development Services, 27
International Parenthood Federation, 39, 47
IUACE, 66

Jay, 23
Joseph, 23

Kapadia, 15, 70
Kapoor, 5, 19, 38, 114
Karnick, 41, 42, 46
Karve, 13, 44
Kashyap, 11, 23-24, 44, 48
Kaur, 93
Kelvin, 58
Knowledge, 65
Kolenda, 15
Korman, 16
Kulkarni, 11, 44
Kumar, 29, 32, 84

Lakshmi Devi, 19
Lakshminarayana, 16, 18
Leslie, 16
Liveright, 29
Lloyd, 22
Locke, 16

MacCracken, 94
Madan, 28
Mahadevan 97
Mahale, 23, 25, 72
Mandelbaum, 70, 97
Mani, 35, 48
Manu, 10
Mathai, 95
Mathew, 20
Mathur, 35
Maygood, 29
Mazumdar, 56
McClelland, 72

Mead, 22, 47
Merh, 4, 5, 38
Methodology, 50-65
  Age, 53-56
  Assessment of variable, 60
  Caste, 56-57
  Family income, 57
  FLE curriculum 62-64
  FLE curriculum schedule, 64
  FLE needs, 53
  FLE needs identification scale, 61
    Reliability of, 61
  General information schedule, 61
  Locale of study, 52, 116
  Marital status, 58
  Operational definition of concepts used, 64
  Place of residence 58
  Relation among independent and dependent variables, 58-60
  Research design, 50-51, 116
  Sample design, 53, 117
  Statistical analysis of data, 64, 118
  Tools for content analysis, 62
  Tools of study, 60-61, 117
  Types of family, 57
  Variables of selection, 53, 117-18, 124
Ministry of Social Welfare, 20
Mohale, 48

National Adult Education Programme, 7, 27, 28, 29-32
  Programme of Action, 31-32
National Committee on Status of Women, 93
National Council of Family Relations of America, 40, 113

National Directorate of Adult Education, 32-33
National Family Planning Programme, 3, 57
National Institute of Rural Development, 20
NFAEP volunteers, 65
Nickell, 57
NTPCCD, 26, 49
Non-formal Adult Education Programme, 64
Norton, 91

Oppenheimer, 91

Pardeck and Pardeck, 24
Pareek, 97
Parikh, 24
Park, 23
Parmar, 44, 95
Poole, 24
Population education, 38

Rajammal, 19
Rajan, 29
Rao, 2, 23, 97
Ramu, 96
Results and discussion, 66-112, 118
  Demographic profile of respondents, 66-75
  Exposure to FLE information, 75-87
  Family income and FLE need perception, 100-09
  FLE programme impact on NAEP participants, 110-12

Identification of FLE needs, 87-93
Socio-economic background, 98-100
Review of literature, 9-49, 115
Achieving emotional independence of parents, 24-27
Establishing one's identity as socially responsible person, 25-27
Preparing for marriage and family life, 25
Selecting and preparing for occupation and economic independence, 25
Conceptual issues on adolescents and FLE, 22-24
Acceptance of changes in body and physique, 23
Achieving satisfying and socially accepted masculine or feminine role, 23
Locating onself as member of one's generation developing more mature relation with one's age mates, 24
Conceptual issues on family significance, 9-13
Family's rights to its environment, 13
Individual rights to have family, 12
Individual rights within family, 12-13
Conceptual issues on non-formal adult education, programme, 28-36
Administrative structure of adult education, 32-34
Literary and numeracy, 34
National Adult Education Programme, 29-32
Social awareness, 34-36
Conceptual issues on transition of Indian family 14-18
Family life education in India, 36-43
Concept and need, 39-43
Historical review of, 36-39
Observations, 43
Rig-veda, 9
Robert, 95
Rodd, 94
Roongruang, 41, 42
Ross, 95-96

Sahay, 14, 44
Saraswathi, 6, 30
Sathe, 25
Saxena, 28
Schvaneveldt, 11, 44
Shah, 43
Sharma, 70
Sigmund, 22, 47
Singh, 22, 43, 45
Smith, 39, 40, 45, 113
Socio-economic background of married women and unmarried adolescent girls, 98-100, 121
Sullivan, 22, 47
Sunberg, 24

Total literacy campaign, 34, 52
Trivedi, 26, 48
Tyler, 24

UNESCO, 27
UNFDA, 27
UNICEF, 27
United Nations Report, 11-12, 18

United Nations Report on Human Rights, 44

Verma, 6, 41, 46, 47
Vidya, 95

Wadia, 2, 27, 35
Walker, 29
WHO, 27
World Conference on Agrarian Reform and Rural Development, 19
World Health Assembly 27

Zaveri, 43
Zilla Saksharata Samithi, 34
Zimmerman, 17-18